MAKING SENSE

a student's guide to writing and style

Margot Northey

Toronto
Oxford University Press
1983

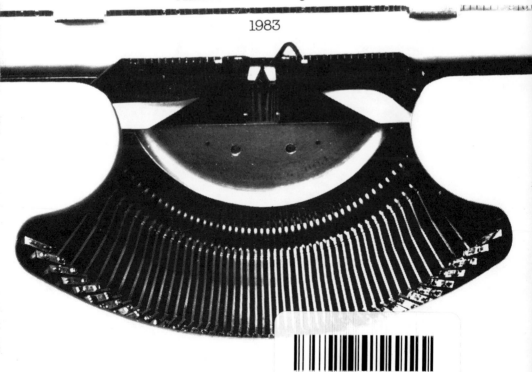

Canadian Cataloguing in Publication Data

Northey, Margot Elizabeth.
  Making sense

Includes index.
ISBN 0-19-540427-0

1. Exposition (Rhetoric).   2. English language –
Rhetoric.   3. Report writing.   I. Title.

LB2369.N67   808'.042   C83-098536-0

Cover photograph by Rudi Christl

© Oxford University Press Canada 1983

4 – 6 5

Printed in Canada by
John Deyell Company

Contents

Acknowledgements

This book was written in response to the needs and requests of the students I have taught in a variety of courses over the years. Many people helped in its preparation. I am first of all grateful to my colleagues at the Erindale campus of the University of Toronto: Professor Tom Adamowski of the Department of English, Myrna Friend of the Library, and Lille Huggett of the Writing Lab, for their help with the chapters on essay writing and documentation in the humanities; Professor Nicholas Collins of the Department of Zoology, Professor Judy Poë of the Department of Chemistry, and Jaleel Ali of the Department of Chemistry, for their suggestions regarding the chapters on lab reports and documentation in the sciences; and Professor L.J. Brooks of the Faculty of Management Studies for his assistance with the chapter on business reports. As well I would like to thank Professor H.J. Rosengarten of the Department of English, University of British Columbia, Professor G. Roseme of the Department of Political Science, Carleton University, and Doreen Lechelt, Assistant Co-ordinator of Reading for the Scarborough Board of Education, for their comments on the manuscript as a whole. I am also grateful to Professor Anderson Silber of the Department of English of the University of Toronto, for encouraging this project, and to the Office of Educational Development of the University of Toronto, for providing funds for the exploratory pamphlets on writing from which this book developed. Finally, I would like to thank Joanna Collins and Fjola Burke for typing the manuscript, and my editors at Oxford University Press, Richard Teleky and Sally Livingston, for their advice and assistance.

Symbols for common errors

NOTE: If any of the following markings appear on one of your essays or reports, consult Chapter 8 or 9, or the Glossary, for help.

agr	agreement of subject and verb
amb	ambiguity
awk	awkwardness
cap	capitalization
cs	comma splice
D	diction
dang	dangling modifier (*or* dm)
frag	sentence fragment
gr	grammar or usage
mod	misplaced modifier
¶	new paragraph
//	parallelism
P	punctuation
quot	quotation marks
ref	pronoun reference
rep	repetition
RO	run-on sentence
sp	spelling
SS	sentence structure
sp inf	split infinitive
sub	subordination
T	tense
trans	transition
⌒	transpose (change order of letters or words)
wdy	wordy
ww	wrong word

A note to the student

Contrary to many students' belief, good writing does not come naturally; even for the best writers it's mostly hard work, following the old formula of ten per cent inspiration and ninety per cent perspiration.

Writing in university or college is not fundamentally different from writing elsewhere. Yet each piece of writing has its own special purposes, and these are what determine its particular substance, shape, and tone. *Making Sense* will examine both the general precepts for effective writing and the special requirements of academic work (especially the essay and report); it will also point out some of the most common errors in student composition and suggest how to avoid or correct them. Written mostly in the form of guidelines rather than strict rules—since few rules are inviolable—this book should help you escape the common pitfalls of student writing and develop confidence through an understanding of basic principles and a mastery of sound techniques.

1
WRITING
and thinking

You are not likely to produce clear writing unless you have first done some clear thinking, and thinking can't be hurried. It follows that the most important step you can take is to leave yourself enough time to think.

Psychologists have shown that we don't always solve a difficult problem by "putting our mind to it"—by determined reasoning. Sometimes when we are stuck it's best to take a break, sleep on it, and let the subconscious or creative part of our brain take over for a while. Very often a period of relaxation will produce a new approach or solution. Just remember that leaving time for creative reflection isn't the same thing as sitting around listening to the stereo until inspiration strikes out of the blue.

INITIAL STRATEGIES

To write is to make choices. Practice makes the decisions easier to come by, but no matter how fluent you become, with each piece of writing you will still have to choose.

You can narrow the field of choice from the start if you realize that you are *not* writing for anybody, anywhere, for no particular reason. In university (or anywhere else), it's always sound strategy to ask yourself two basic questions: "What is the purpose of this piece of writing?" and "What is the reader like?" Your first reaction may be "Well, I'm writing for my teacher to satisfy a course requirement." But that's not specific enough. To be useful, your answers have to be precise.

Think about the purpose

Your purpose may be any one or two of several possibilities:
- to show that you understand certain terms or theories;
- to show that you can do independent research;
- to apply a specific theory to new material;
- to provide information;
- to show your knowledge of a topic or text;
- to show that you can think critically or creatively.

Certainly an assignment designed to see if you have read and understood specific material calls for a different approach from one that's meant to test your critical thinking or research skills. If you don't determine the exact purpose, you may find yourself working at cross purposes—and wasting a lot of time.

Think about the reader

Thinking about the reader does *not* mean playing up to the teacher. To convince a particular person that your own views are sound, you have to consider his or her way of thinking. If you are writing a paper on Israeli communes for a sociology professor, obviously your analysis will be different from what it would be if you were writing for an economics or history professor. You will have to make specific decisions about the terms you should explain, the background information you should supply, and the details you need to convince that particular reader. In the same way, if your reader supports the idea of a common market between Canada and the United States and you intend to propose higher tariffs, you will have to anticipate any arguments that may be raised, in order to answer them. If you don't know who will be reading your paper—your professor, your tutorial leader, or a marker—just imagine someone intelligent, knowledgeable, and interested, skeptical enough to question your ideas but flexible enough to adopt them if your evidence is convincing.

Think about the length

Before you start writing, you will also need to think about the length of your assignment in relation to the time you have available to spend on it. If both the topic and the length are prescribed, it should be fairly easy for you to assess the level of detail required and the amount of research you need to do. If only the length is prescribed, that restriction will help you decide how broad or how narrow a topic you should choose (see p. 8).

Think about the tone

In everyday writing to friends you probably take a casual tone, but academic writing is usually more formal. The exact degree of formality required will depend on the kind of assignment and instruction you have been given. In some cases—say, if your psychology or philosophy professor asks you to express yourself freely and personally in a journal—you may well be able to use an informal style. Essays and reports, however, require a more formal tone. What kind of style is too informal for most academic work? Here are the main signs:

Use of slang

Although the occasional slang word or phrase may be useful for special effect, frequent use of slang is not acceptable. The reason is that slang expressions are usually regional and short-lived: they may mean different things to different groups at different times. (Just think of how widely the meanings of *hot* and *cool* can vary, depending on the circumstances.)

Excessive use of first-person pronouns

Since a formal essay is not a personal outpouring, you want to keep it from becoming *I*-centred. It's certainly acceptable to use the occasional first-person pronoun, and your reader will obviously want to know your opinions—as long as they are backed by evidence. Still, you should avoid the *I think* or *in my view* approach when the fact or argument speaks for itself. If the choice, however, is between using *I* and creating a tangle of passive constructions, it's almost always better to choose *I*. (A hint: when you do use *I*, it will be less noticeable if you place it in the middle of the sentence rather than at the beginning.)

Frequent use of contractions

Generally speaking, contractions such as *can't* and *isn't* are not suitable for academic writing, although they may be fine for letters or other informal kinds of writing—for example, this handbook. The problem with trying to avoid excessive informality is that you may be tempted to go to the other extreme. If your writing sounds stiff or pompous, you may be using too many high-flown phrases, long words, or passive constructions (see Chapter 7).

2
WRITING
an essay

If you are one of the many students who dread writing an academic essay, you will find that following a few simple steps in planning and organizing will make the task easier—and the result better.

THE PLANNING STAGE

Some students claim they can write essays without any planning at all. On the rare occasions when they succeed, their writing is usually not as spontaneous as it seems: in fact, they have thought or talked a good deal about the subject in advance, and come to the task with some ready-made ideas. More often, trying to write a lengthy essay without planning just leads them to frustration. They get stuck in the middle and don't know how to finish, or suddenly realize that they are rambling off in all directions.

In contrast, most writers say that the planning, or pre-writing, stage is the most important part of the whole process. Certainly the evidence shows that poor planning usually leads to disorganized writing; in the majority of students' essays the single greatest improvement would not be better research or better grammar, but better organization.

This insistence on planning doesn't rule out exploratory writing (see p. 14). Many people find that the act of writing itself is the best way to generate ideas or overcome writer's block; the hard decisions about organization come after they've put something down on the page. Whether you organize before or after you begin to write, however, at some point you need to plan.

Reading primary material

Primary material is the direct evidence—usually books or articles—on which you will base your essay. Surprising as it may seem, the best way to begin working with this material is to give it a fast initial skim. Don't just start reading from cover to cover: first look at the table of contents, scan the index, and read the preface or introduction to get a sense of the author's purpose and plan. Getting an overview will allow you to focus your questions for a more purposeful and analytic second reading. Make no mistake: a superficial reading is *not* all you need. You still have to work through the material carefully a second time. But an initial skim followed by a focused second reading will give you a much more thorough understanding than one slow plod ever will.

A warning about secondary sources

Always be sure you have a firm grasp of the primary material before you turn to secondary sources (commentaries on or analyses of the primary source). Some instructors discourage secondary reading in introductory courses because they know the dangers of relying too heavily on it. If you turn to commentaries as a way around the difficulty of understanding the primary source, you may be overwhelmed by the weight of authority, and your essay will be trite and second-hand. Your interpretation could even be downright wrong, since at this stage you may not know enough about a subject to be able to evaluate the commentary. Secondary sources are an important part of research, but they can never substitute for your own active reading of the primary material.

Analyse your subject: ask questions

Some instructors ask students to choose their own essay topics, and others simply suggest subject areas. In either case, since a subject area is bound to be too broad for an essay topic, you will have to analyse it in order to find a way of limiting it. The best way of analysing is to ask questions that will lead to useful answers.

How do you form that kind of question? Journalists approach their stories through a five-question formula: *who? what? where? when? why?* You could apply the same formula to aspects of your subject, and add *how?* For example, starting with the question *what?* and applying it to a work of fiction, you might ask "What contrasts of character can one find?''; "What role do the minor characters play?''; "What are the good or evil qualities of the characters?'' *How* and *why* questions are often the most productive, since they take you beyond information-gathering and force you to analyse and interpret. If you are considering the Canadian constitution, for example, you might ask "How are the courts likely to be affected by the new constitution?'' "Why was education left to the provinces?''

Try the three-C approach

A more systematic scheme for analysing a subject is the three-C approach. It asks three basic questions about *components*, *change*, and *context*:

What are the components of the subject? In other words, how might it be broken down into smaller elements? This question forces you to take a close look at the subject and helps you avoid over-simplification. Suppose that your assignment is to discuss the policies of Mackenzie King. After asking yourself about components, you might decide that you can split the subject into (1) domestic policies and (2) foreign policies. Alternatively, you might divide it into (1) economic policies, (2) social policies, and (3) political policies. Then, since these components themselves are fairly broad, you might break them down further. Economic policies might be split into fiscal and monetary policies; political policies could be split into relations with the provinces and relations with other countries.

What features of the subject reflect change? For example, did Mackenzie King's policies in a certain area alter over a period of years? Did he express contradictory views in different documents? What caused changes in policy? What were the effects of these changes?

What is the context of this subject? Into what particular school of thought or tradition does it fit? What are the similarities and differences between this subject and related ones? For example, how do Mackenzie King's policies compare with those of other Liberal Prime Ministers? With Conservative policies?

General as most of these questions are, you will find that they stimulate more specific questions—and thoughts—about the material, from which you can choose your topic and formulate a thesis. Remember that the ability to ask intelligent questions is one of the most important, though often underrated, skills that you can develop for any work, in university and outside.

Analysing a prescribed topic

Even if the topic of your essay is supplied by your instructor, you still need to analyse it carefully. Try underlining key words to make sure that you don't neglect anything. Distinguish the main focus from subordinate concerns. A common error in dealing with prescribed topics is to emphasize one portion while giving short shrift to another. Give each part its proper due—and make sure that you actually do what the instructions tell you to do. To *discuss* is not the same as to *evaluate* or *trace*; to *compare* means to show differences as well as similarities. These verbs tell you how to approach the topic; don't confuse them.

Develop a hypothesis

Not all essays are arguments, nor do they all require a specific thesis. Yet most students find it helpful to think of an academic essay as a way of demonstrating or proving a point, since the argumentative form is the easiest to organize and the most likely to produce forceful writing. A hypothesis is nothing more than a working thesis—an intended line of argument which you are free to change at any stage of your planning. It works as a linchpin, holding together your information and ideas as you organize. It will help you to define your intentions, make your research more selective, and focus your essay.

At some point in the writing process you will probably want to make your hypothesis into an explicit thesis statement that can appear in your introduction. In any case, you should take the time to work out your thesis carefully. Use a complete sentence to express it, and above all, make sure that it is *limited*, *unified*, and *exact*.[1]

Make it limited

A limited thesis is one that is narrow enough to be workable. Suppose, for example, that your general subject is the Social Credit party in Canada. Such a subject is much too broad to be handled properly in an essay of one or two thousand words: you must limit it in some way and create a line of argument for which you can supply adequate supporting evidence. Following the analytic questioning process, you might find that you want to restrict it by time: "The Social Credit party in the 1970s was indistinguishable in its monetary policies from the Conservative party." Or you might prefer to limit it by geography: "The development of the Social Credit party in British Columbia had less to do with its policies than with its political opportunities."

To take an example from literature, suppose that your general subject for a two-thousand-word essay is the work of Hugh MacLennan. You might want to limit it by discussing a prominent theme in one or two novels: "Although MacLennan exposes the dark side of religion in *Each Man's Son*, he also reveals a yearning for spiritual wholeness." Or you could focus on some aspect of characterization: "In *Each Man's Son* and *The Watch That Ends the Night*, MacLennan creates drama through his contrast of character types." Whatever the discipline or subject, make sure that your topic is restricted enough that you can explore it in depth.

Make it unified

To be unified, your thesis must have one controlling idea. Beware of the double-headed thesis: "In his term as President of the United States, Lyndon Johnson introduced many social programs, but the Vietnam War issue led to his downfall." What is the controlling idea here? The success of Johnson's social programs, or the reason for his downfall? The essay should focus on one or the other. It is possible to have two or more related ideas in a thesis, but only if one of them is clearly in control, with all the other ideas subordinated to it: "Despite criticism from various regions in Canada, the CBC is an instrument of national unity."

Make it exact

It's important, especially in a thesis, to avoid vague terms such as *interesting* and *significant*, as in "Helmut Schmidt was Germany's most interesting Chancellor." Does *interesting* mean *effective* or *daring* in his policies, or does it mean personally *charming*? Don't say simply "Sheila Watson's use of symbols is an important feature of her writing" when you can be more precise about the work you are discussing, the kind of symbols you've found there, and exactly what they do: "In *The Double Hook*, Sheila Watson adapts traditional symbols from Christian and Indian mythology to underscore the theme of spiritual death and regeneration." Remember to be as specific as possible in creating a thesis, in order to focus your essay. Don't just make an assertion—give the main reasons for it. Instead of saying simply "Many westerners are resentful of central Canada" and leaving it at that, add an explanation: ". . . because of historic grievances, such as tariffs and freight rates, and contemporary issues such as the energy policy and the new constitution.'' If these details make your thesis stylistically cumbersome, don't worry. A thesis is only a planning device, something to guide the organization of your ideas. The wording doesn't have to be the same in your final essay.

Research your topic

If your topic requires more facts or evidence than the primary material provides, or if you want to know other people's opinions on the subject, you will need to visit the library for research. Some students like to read around in the subject area before they decide on an essay topic; for them, the thesis comes after the exploration. You may find this approach useful for some essays, but generally it's better to narrow your scope and plan a tentative thesis before you turn to secondary sources—you'll save time and produce a more original essay.

Explore the library

The importance of getting to know your way around a library can't be stressed enough. You don't want to be so overwhelmed by its size and complexity that you either scrimp on required research or waste time and energy trying to find information. Remember that most academic libraries have orientation seminars specifically designed to show you where and how to find what you want—how to use a card catalogue, for example. Take advantage of these services. Librarians will be glad to show you the bibliographies, indices, and other reference books for your field of study. Once you are familiar with these basic sources you will be able to check systematically for available material.

Taking good notes

Finding your research material is one thing; taking notes that are dependable and easy to use is another. With time you will develop your own best method, but for a start you might try the index-card system. Record each new idea or piece of evidence on a separate card (see p. 11); the number you need will obviously depend on the range and type of your research. When you've finished with your note-taking, you can then easily arrange the cards in the order in which you will use them.

ARNOLD J. TOYNBEE, *A Study of History.*
Abridgement of vols. 1-1V by D.C. SOMERVELL
(New York and London: Oxford Univ. Press, 1946).

Says 20th Century follows "typical pattern of
a time of troubles: a breakdown, a rally and
a second relapse" (p. 553).

Index Card

Whatever method you follow, remember that exact records are essential for proper footnotes:

1. For every entry check that the bibliographic details are complete, including the name of the author, title, place and date of publication, and page number, as well as the library call number. Nothing is more frustrating than using a piece of information in an essay only to find that you aren't sure where it came from. If you take several ideas from one source, it helps to put the main bibliographic details about the author and work on one card, and then use a separate card for each particular idea or theory.
2. Check that quotations are copied precisely.
3. Include page numbers for every reference, even if you paraphrase or summarize the idea rather than copy it word for word.

A warning about plagiarism

Plagiarism is a form of stealing; as with other offences against the law, ignorance is no excuse. The way to avoid it is to give credit where credit is due. If you are using someone else's idea, acknowledge it, even if you have changed the wording or just summarized the main points. You may give credit either directly in the text (''As Toynbee says, . . .'') or in a footnote. (For footnote style, see Chapter 10.) Don't be afraid that your work will seem weaker if you acknowledge the ideas of others. On the contrary, it will be all the more convincing: serious academic treatises are almost always built on the work of preceding scholars.

Where should you draw the line on acknowledgements? As a rule you don't need to give credit for anything that's common knowledge. You wouldn't footnote the well-known sayings of Jesus, for example, or lines from ''O Canada,'' or the date of Confederation; however, you should acknowledge any clever turn of phrase that is neither well known nor your own. And always document any unfamiliar fact or claim—statistical or otherwise—or one that's open to question.

Creating an outline

Individual writers differ in their need for a formal plan. Some say that they never have an outline, and others maintain they can't write without one; most fall somewhere in between. Since organization is such a common problem, though, it's a good idea to know how to draw up an effective plan. Of course, the exact form it takes will depend on the pattern you use to develop your ideas—whether you are defining, classifying, or comparing, for example (see pp. 14-17).

If you have special problems with organizing material, your outline should be formal, in complete sentences. On the other hand, if your mind is naturally logical, you may find it's enough just to jot down a few words on a scrap of paper. For most students, an informal but well-organized outline in point form is the most useful model:

THESIS: When Trudeau first came to power, his style was seen as an enormous asset, but by the '80s the same style was increasingly seen as a liability.

    I. Trudeau's early style perceived in positive light
      A. Charismatic
        1. Public adulation: ''Trudeaumania''
        2. Media awe
      B. Intellectual

      C. Tough
         1. Handling of journalists
         2. Handling of Quebec
      D. Anti-establishment
         1. Swinging lifestyle
         2. Disregard for government traditions
  II. Later reversal: Trudeau's image becomes negative
      A. Irritating
         1. Public opinion polls
         2. Media disenchantment
      B. Out of touch with economic reality
      C. Confrontationist
         1. With individual dissenters
         2. With Premiers
         3. With Opposition leaders
      D. Arrogant
         1. Extravagant lifestyle in time of recession
         2. Autocratic approach to governing

The guidelines for this kind of outline are simple:

Code your categories. Use different sets of markings to establish the relative importance of your entries. The example here moves from roman numerals to letters to arabic numbers, but you could use another system.

Categorize according to importance. Make sure that only items of equal value are put in equivalent categories. Give major points more weight than minor ones.

Check lines of connection. Make sure that each of the main categories is directly linked to the central thesis; then see that each sub-category is directly linked to the larger category that contains it. Checking these lines of connection is the best way of preventing essay muddle.

Be consistent. In arranging your points, be consistent. You may choose to move from the most important point to the least important, or vice versa, as long as you follow the same order every time.

Use parallel wording. Phrasing each entry in a similar way will make it easier to be consistent in your presentation.

One final word: be prepared to change your outline at any time in the writing process. An outline is not meant to put an iron clamp on your thinking, but to relieve anxiety about where you're heading. A careful outline prevents frustration and dead ends—that ''I'm stuck, where can I go from here?'' feeling. But since the very act of writing will usually generate new ideas, you should be ready to modify your original plan. Just remember that any new outline must have the consistency and clear connections required for a unified essay.

THE WRITING STAGE

Writing the first draft

Rather than labouring for excellence from scratch, most writers find it easier to write the first draft as quickly as possible and do extensive revisions later. However you begin, you can't expect the first draft to be the final copy. Skilled writers know that revising is a necessary part of the writing process, and that the care taken with revisions makes the difference between a mediocre essay and a good one.

You don't need to write all parts of the essay in the same order in which they are to appear in the final copy. In fact, many students find the introduction the hardest part to write. If you face the first blank page with a growing sense of paralysis, try leaving the introduction until later, and start with the first idea in your outline. If you feel so intimidated that you haven't even been able to draw up an outline, you might try John Trimble's approach and charge right ahead with any kind of beginning—even a simple ''My first thoughts on this subject are . . . ''.[2] Instead of sharpening pencils or running out for a snack, try to get going. Don't worry about grammar or wording; scratch out pages or throw them away if you must. Remember, the object is to get your writing juices flowing.

Of course, you can't expect this kind of exploratory writing to resemble the first draft that follows an outline. You will probably need to do a great deal more changing and reorganizing, but at least you will have the relief of seeing words on a page to work with. Many experienced writers—and not only those with writer's block—find this the most productive way to proceed.

Developing your ideas: some common patterns

The way you develop your ideas will depend on your essay topic, and topics can vary enormously. Even so, most essays follow one or another of a handful of basic organizational patterns. Here's how to use each pattern effectively.

1. Defining

Sometimes a whole essay is an extended definition, explaining the meaning of a term that is complicated, controversial, or simply important to your field of study: for example, *nationalism* in political science, or *monetarism* in economics, or *existentialism* in philosophy. More often, perhaps, you may want to begin a detailed discussion of a topic by defining a key term, and then shift to a different organizational pattern. In either case, make your definition exact. It should be broad enough to include all the things that belong in the category and at the same time narrow enough to exclude things that don't belong. A good definition builds a kind of verbal fence around a word, herding together all the members of the class and cutting off all outsiders.

For any discussion of a term that goes beyond a bare definition, you should, of course, give concrete illustrations or examples; depending on the nature of your essay, these could vary in length from one or two sentences to several paragraphs or even pages. If you are defining monetarism, for instance, you would probably want to discuss at some length the theories of leading monetarists.

In an extended definition, it's also useful to point out the differences between the term and any other that is connected with it or often confused with it. For instance, if you are defining *pathos* you might want to distinguish it from *tragedy*; if you are defining *common law*, you might want to distinguish it from *statute law*.

2. Classifying

Classifying means dividing something into its separate parts according to a given principle of selection. The principle or criterion may vary; you could classify crops, for example, according to how they grow (above the ground or below the ground), how long they take to mature, or what climatic conditions they require; members of a given population might be classified according to age group, occupation, income, and so on. If you are organizing your essay by a system of classification, remember the following:

- All members of a class must be accounted for. If any are left over, you need to alter some categories or add more.
- Categories can be divided into subcategories. You should consider using subcategories if there are significant differences within

a category. If, for instance, you are classifying the work force according to occupation, you might want to create subcategories according to income level or sex.

• Any subcategory should contain at least two items.

3. Explaining a process

This kind of organization shows how something works or has worked, whether it be the weather cycle, the process of justice, or the stages in a political or military campaign. The important point to remember is to be systematic, to break down the process into a series of steps or stages. Although at times it will vary, most often your order will be chronological, in which case you should see that the sequence is accurate and easy to follow. Whatever the arrangement, you can generally make the process easier to follow if you start a new paragraph for each new stage.

4. Tracing causes or effects

A cause-or-effect analysis is really a particular kind of process discussion, in which certain events are shown to have led to or resulted from other events. Usually you are explaining *why* something happened. The main warning here is to avoid over-simplifying. If you are tracing causes, distinguish between a direct cause and a contributing cause, between what is a condition of something happening and what is merely a correlation or coincidence. For example, if you find that both the age of the average driver in Canada and the number of accidents caused by drunk drivers are increasing, you cannot jump to the conclusion that older drivers are the cause of the increase in drunk-driving accidents. Similarly, you must be sure that the result you mention is a genuine product of the event or action.

5. Comparing

One point sometimes forgotten is that comparing things means showing differences as well as similarities—even if the topic does not say "compare and contrast." The easiest method for comparison—though not always the best—is to discuss the first subject in the comparison thoroughly and then move on to the second:

Subject *X:*   Point 1

Point 2

Point 3

Subject *Y:*   Point 1
Point 2
Point 3

The problem with this kind of comparison is that it often sounds like two separate essays slapped together. To be successful you must integrate the two subjects, first in your introduction (by putting them both in a single context) and again in your conclusion, where you should bring together the important points you have made about each. When discussing the second subject, try to refer repeatedly to your findings about the first subject (''unlike *X, Y* does such and such''). This method may be the wisest choice if the subjects for comparison seem so unlike that it is hard to create similar categories by which to discuss them—if the points you are making about *X* are of a different type than the points you are making about *Y.*

If it is possible to find similar criteria or categories for discussing both subjects, however, the comparison will be more effective if you organize it like this:

Category 1:   Subject *X*
Subject *Y*
Category 2:   Subject *X*
Subject *Y*
Category 3:   Subject *X*
Subject *Y*

Because this kind of comparison is more tightly integrated, the reader can more readily see the similarities and differences between the subjects. As a result, the essay is likely to be more forceful.

Introductions

The beginning of an essay has a dual purpose: to indicate both the topic and your approach to it, and to whet your reader's interest in what you have to say. One effective way of introducing a topic is to place it in a context—to supply a kind of backdrop that will put it in perspective. You step back a pace and discuss the area into which your topic fits, and then gradually lead into your specific field of discussion. Sheridan Baker[3] calls this the funnel approach (see p. 19). For example, suppose that your topic is the growing moral maturity of Brian O'Connal in W.O. Mitchell's *Who Has Seen the Wind?* You might begin with a more general discussion of growing up in the west, or the movement from innocence to experience in other novels. A funnel opening is applicable to almost any kind of essay.

It's a good idea to try to catch your reader's interest right from the start—you know from your own reading how a dull beginning can put you off. The fact that your instructor must read on anyway makes no difference. If a reader has to get through thirty or forty similar essays, it's all the more important for yours to stand out. A funnel opening isn't the only way to catch the reader's attention. Here are three of the most common leads:

The quotation. This approach works especially well when the quotation is taken from the person or work that you will be discussing.

The question. A rhetorical question will only annoy the reader if it's commonplace or the answer is obvious, but a thought-provoking question can make a strong opening. Just be sure that you answer the question in your essay.

The anecdote or telling fact. This is the kind of concrete lead that journalists often use to grab their readers' attention. Save it for your least formal essays—and remember that the incident must really highlight the ideas you are going to discuss.

Whatever your lead, it must relate to your topic: never sacrifice relevance for originality. Finally, whether your introduction is one paragraph or several, make sure that by the end of it your reader clearly knows the direction you are taking.

Conclusions

Endings can be painful—sometimes for the reader as much as for the writer. Too often, the feeling that one ought to say something profound and memorable produces the kind of prose that suggests violins throbbing in the background. You know the sort of thing:

> Clearly the symbolism of Four Quartets is both intellectually and emotionally stimulating. Through it Eliot has produced poetry of lasting significance which will inspire readers for generations to come.

Why is this embarrassing? Because it's phony—a grab-bag of clichés.

Experienced editors often say that many articles and essays would be better without their final paragraphs: in other words, when you have finished what you want to say, the only thing to do is stop. This advice works best for short essays, where you need to keep the central point firmly in the foreground and don't need to remind the reader of it. For longer pieces, where you have developed a number of ideas or a complex line of argument, you should provide a sense of closure. Readers welcome an ending that helps to tie the ideas together; they don't like to feel they've been left dangling. And since the final impression is often the most lasting, it's in your interest to finish strongly. Simply restating your thesis or summarizing what you have already said isn't forceful enough. What are the other options?

The inverse funnel. The simplest and most basic conclusion is one that restates the thesis *in different words* and then discusses its implications. Sheridan Baker calls this the inverse funnel approach, as opposed to the funnel approach of the opening paragraph.[4]

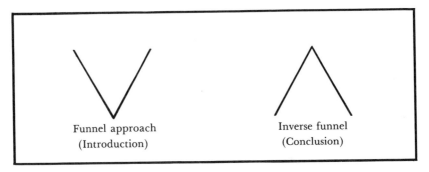

Funnel approach
(Introduction)

Inverse funnel
(Conclusion)

One danger in moving to a wider perspective is that you may try to embrace too much. When a conclusion expands too far it tends to lose focus and turn into an empty cliché, like the conclusion in the preceding example. It's always better to discuss specific implications than to leap into the thin air of vague generalities.

The new angle. A variation of the basic inverse funnel approach is to reintroduce your argument with a new twist. Suggesting some fresh angle can add excitement to your ending. Beware of injecting an entirely new idea, though, or one that's only loosely connected to your original argument: the result could be jarring or even off-topic.

The full circle. If your introduction is based on an anecdote, a question, or a startling fact, you can complete the circle by referring to it again in relation to some of the insights revealed in the main body of your essay.

The stylistic flourish. Some of the most successful conclusions end on a strong stylistic note. Try varying the sentence structure: if most of your sentences are long and complex, make the last one short and punchy, or vice versa. Sometimes you can dramatize your idea with a striking phrase or colourful image. When you are writing your essay, keep your eyes open and your ears tuned for fresh ways of putting things, and save the best for the end.

None of these approaches to endings is exclusive, of course. You may even find that several of them can be combined in a single essay.

THE EDITING STAGE

Often the best writer in a class is not the one who can dash off a fluent first draft, but the one who is the best editor. To edit your work well you need to see it as the reader will; you have to distinguish between what you meant to say and what is actually on the page. For this reason it's a good idea to leave some time between drafts, so that when you begin to edit you will be looking at the writing afresh rather than reviewing it from memory. Now's the time to go to a movie or play some squash—do anything that will take your mind off your work. Without this distancing period you can become so involved that it's hard to see your paper objectively.

Editing doesn't mean simply checking your work for errors in grammar or spelling. It means looking at the piece *as a whole* to see if the ideas are (1) well organized, (2) well documented, and (3) well expressed. It may mean adding some paragraphs, deleting others, and shifting still others around. It very likely means adding, deleting, and shifting sentences and phrases. Experienced writers may be able to check several aspects of their work at the same time, but if you are inexperienced or in doubt about your writing, it's best to look at the organization of the ideas before you tackle sentence structure, diction, style, and documentation.

What follows is a check-list of questions to ask yourself as you begin editing. Far from all-inclusive, it focuses on the first step: examining the organization. You probably won't want to check through your work separately for each question: you can group some together and overlook others, depending on your own strengths and weaknesses as a writer.

Preliminary editing check-list

1. Are the purpose and approach of this essay evident from the beginning?
2. Are all sections of the paper relevant to the topic?
3. Is the organization logical?
4. Are the ideas sufficiently developed? Is there enough evidence, explanation, and illustration?

5. Would an educated person who hasn't read the primary material understand everything I'm saying? Should I clarify some parts or add any explanatory material?
6. In presenting my argument, do I take into account opposing arguments or evidence?
7. Do my paragraph divisions give coherence to my ideas? Do I use them to cluster similar ideas and signal changes of idea?
8. Do any parts of the essay seem disjointed? Should I add more transitional words or logical indicators to make the sequence of ideas easier to follow?

Another approach would be to devise your own check-list based on the faults of previous assignments. This is particularly useful when you move from the overview to the close focus on sentence structure, diction, punctuation, spelling, and style. If you have a particular weak area—for example, irrelevant evidence, faulty logic, or run-on sentences—you should give it special attention. Keeping a personal check-list will save you from repeating the same old mistakes.

A few words about appearance

We've all been told not to judge a book by its cover, but the very warning suggests that we have a natural tendency to do so. Readers of essays find the same thing. A well-typed, visually appealing essay creates a receptive reader and, fairly or unfairly, often gets a higher mark than a hand-written one—especially if the hand-writing is messy or hard to read. Whenever possible, therefore, type your essay. If you can't type or afford to hire a typist, take special care that your script is neat and easy to read. If your hand-writing is poor, print. In any case, double-space your lines and leave wide margins on sides, top, and bottom, framing the script in white. Leave three centimetres at least at the sides and top and four centimetres at the bottom, so that the reader has ample space to write comments. Number each page at the top right-hand corner, and provide a neat, well-spaced cover page which includes the title, your name, and the name of your instructor and course. Good looks won't substitute for good thinking, but they will certainly enhance it.

NOTES

[1] James McCrimmon, *Writing With a Purpose*, 6th ed. (Boston: Houghton Mifflin Co., 1976), 18.
[2] John R. Trimble, *Writing with Style: Conversations on the Art of Writing* (Englewood Cliffs, N.J.: Prentice-Hall, Inc., 1975), 11.
[3] Sheridan Baker, *The Practical Stylist*, 5th ed. (New York: Harper & Row Pubs. Inc., 1981), 24-5.
[4] *Ibid.*

3
WRITING
a book report

The term *book report* covers a variety of writing assignments, from a simple summary of a book's contents to a sophisticated literary review. In between is the kind that you will most often be asked to produce: an analytic report containing some evaluation. The following guidelines cover the three basic kinds. Before you begin your assignment, be sure to check with your instructor to find out exactly which type is expected.

THE INFORMATIVE BOOK REPORT OR SUMMARY

Your purpose in this kind of report is to summarize a book briefly and coherently. It's not a complicated task, but it does call on your ability to get to the heart of things, to separate what is important from what is not—a useful skill both in school and on the job. Aside from some pertinent publication information, all a simple informative report needs is an accurate summary of the book's contents.

Writing guidelines

Determine the author's purpose

An author writes a book for a reason: to cast some new light on a subject, to propose a new theory, or to bring together the existing knowledge in a field. Whatever the purpose, you have to discover it if you want to understand what guided the author's selection and arrangement of material. The best way to find out what the author intends to do is to check the table of contents, preface, and introduction.

Skim-read the book first

As noted earlier (p. 6), a quick overview of the book's contents will show you what the author considers most important and what kind of evidence he or she presents. The details will be much more understandable once you know where the book as a whole is going.

Reread carefully and take notes

A second, more thorough reading will be the basis of your note-taking. Since you have already determined the relative importance that the author gives to various ideas, you can be selective and avoid getting bogged down in a welter of unimportant detail. Just be sure that you don't neglect any crucial passages or controversial claims.

When you are taking notes try to condense the ideas. Don't take them down word for word, and don't simply paraphrase them. You will have a much firmer grasp of the material if you resist the temptation to quote; force yourself to interpret. This approach will also help to make your report concise—remember, you want to be brief as well as clear. Condensing the material as you take notes will ensure that your report is a true summary, not just a string of quotations or paraphrases.

Pull your notes together to form a clear summary of the contents

Give the same relative emphasis to each area that the author does. Don't just list the topics in the book or the conclusions reached: discriminate between primary ideas and secondary ones.

Follow the book's order of presentation. Strictly speaking, a simple summary need not do so, but it's usually safer to follow the author's lead. That way your summary will be a clear reflection of the original.

Follow the logical chain of the arguments. Don't leave any confusing holes. You won't be able to cover every detail, of course, but you must make sure to trace all the main arguments in such a way that they make logical sense.

Include the key evidence supporting the author's arguments. Without some supporting details, your reader will have no way of assessing the strength of the conclusions.

Tailor the length to fit your needs. A summary can be any length, from one page to six or seven. It depends less on the length of the original material than on your purpose. If the report is an assignment, find out how long your instructor wants it to be. If it's for personal reference only, you will have to decide how much detail you want to have on hand.

Read and revise your report to make sure it's coherent

Summaries can often seem choppy or disconnected because so much of the original is left out. Use linking words and phrases (see p. 61) to help create a flow and give your writing a sense of logical development. Careful paragraph division will also help to frame the various sections of the summary. If the report is for a science or social science course, you can probably use headings as well to identify sections.

Include publication details

Details about the book (publisher, place and date of publication, and number of pages) must appear somewhere in your report, whether at the beginning or at the end. Follow the guidelines in Chapter 10. Separate these publication details from your discussion by a triple space.

THE ANALYTIC BOOK REPORT

An analytic book report—sometimes called a book review—not only summarizes the main ideas in a book but at the same time evaluates them. You are best to begin with an introduction, then follow with your summary and evaluation. Publication details can come either at the beginning or at the end.

Writing guidelines

Introduction

You should provide all the background information necessary for a reader who is not familiar with the book. Here are some of the questions you might consider:
- What is the book about?
- What is the author's purpose? What kind of audience is he or she writing for? How is the topic limited? Is the central theme or argument stated or only implied?
- How does this book relate to others in its special field of interest? To other aspects of the same field?

- What are the author's background and reputation? What other books or articles has he or she written?
- Are there any special circumstances connected with the writing of this book?
- What sources has the author used?

Not all of these questions will be applicable to every book. Nevertheless, an introduction that answers some of them will put your reader in a much better position to appreciate what you have to say.

Summary

Obviously you cannot analyse a book without discussing its contents: the basic steps are the same as for the simple book summary. You may choose to present a condensed version of the book's contents as a separate section, to be followed by your evaluation; or you may prefer to integrate the two, assessing the author's arguments as you present them.

Evaluation

In evaluating the book, you might ask some of the following questions:
- How is the book organized? Are the divisions valid? Does the author give short shrift to certain areas? Is anything left out?
- What kind of assumptions does the author make in presenting the material? Are they stated or implied? Are they valid?
- Does the book accomplish what it sets out to do? Does the author's position change in the course of the book? Are there any contradictions or weak spots in the arguments? Does the author recognize those weaknesses or omissions? Remember that your job is not only to analyse the contents of the book, but to indicate its strengths and weaknesses.
- What kind of evidence is presented to support the author's ideas? Is it reliable and up to date? Are any of the data distorted or misinterpreted? Could the same evidence be used to support a different case? Does the book leave out any important evidence that might weaken its case? Is the author's position convincing?
- Does the author agree or disagree with other writers who have dealt with the same material or problem? In what respects?
- Is the book clearly written and interesting to read? Is the writing repetitious? Too detailed? Not detailed enough? Is the style clear? Or is it plodding, or jargonish, or flippant?

- Does the book raise issues that need further exploration? Does it present any challenges or leave unfinished business for the author or other scholars to pick up?
- To what extent would you recommend this book? What effect has it had on you?

THE LITERARY REVIEW

The literary review is a variation of the analytic book report. Although literature is its most frequent subject, it may deal with a wide range of topics, from art and music to the social sciences. The term ''literary'' refers to the presentation rather than to the material discussed: the review should stand on its own merit as an attractive piece of writing.

The advantage of a literary review is the freedom it allows you in both content and presentation. You may emphasize any aspect you like, as long as you leave your reader with a basic understanding of what the book is about. In most cases, your purpose is simply to provide a graceful introduction to the work based on a personal assessment of its most intriguing—or annoying—features. Just don't be too personal: some reviewers end up telling us more about themselves than about the book. Although a literary review is usually less comprehensive than an analytic report, it should always be thoughtful, and your judgement must never be superficial.

The best way of learning how to write good literary reviews is to read some of them. Check the book review sections of a magazine such as *Saturday Night*, a journal like *Canadian Forum*, or the weekend edition of the *Globe and Mail* to see different approaches. Pay particular attention to the various techniques that reviewers use to catch the reader's interest and hold it. The basic rule is to reinforce your comments with specific details from the book; concrete examples will add authenticity and life to your review.

4
WRITING
a lab report

Students in the sciences and social sciences are often asked to report formally on the results of scientific experiments. Although lab reports generally conform to a basic format, each discipline (chemistry, physics, biology, psychology, etc.) has slightly different requirements.

Any kind of academic writing should be clear, concise, and forceful, but for scientific writing there is one more imperative: be objective. Scientists are interested in exact information, in the orderly presentation of factual evidence to support theories or claims. You must never allow your preconceived opinions or biases, or even expectations, to get in the way of the facts or distort them. You must present your information in such a way that anyone who reads your report or attempts to duplicate your procedure would be likely to reach the same conclusions that you did.

PURPOSE AND READER

As an undergraduate, you will most often write lab reports to demonstrate that you understand a theory or process, or that you know how to test a certain hypothesis. Since your reader is your instructor, you can assume that he or she will be familiar with scientific terms; therefore you do not need to define or explain them. You can also assume that your reader will be on the look-out for any weaknesses in methodology or analysis and any omissions of important data. Usually you will be expected to give details of your calculations, but even when all you have been asked to give is the results of your calculations, you should include any experimental uncertainty that might affect them.

FORMAT

Since the information in scientific reports must be easy for the reader to find and assess, it should be grouped into separate sections, each with a heading. One of the differences between writing lab reports and writing essays is that in a report you should use headings and subheadings whenever possible, as well as graphs, tables, or diagrams. Most lab reports follow a standard order:

1. Title page
2. Abstract or summary
3. Introduction
4. Materials
5. Method
6. Results
7. Discussion
8. Conclusion

Depending on the amount of information you have in each area, you may choose to combine certain sections.

Title page

The first page of the report is your title page. It should include the title of the experiment, the date it was performed, your name, and the date of submission; for practical purposes it should also include the name of your course and instructor. Your title should be brief but informative, clearly indicating the subject and scope of your experiment. Avoid meaningless phrases, such as ''A study of . . .'' or ''Observations on . . .''; simply state *what* it is that you are studying.

Abstract

Also known as a summary, the abstract appears on a separate page following the title page. It is a brief summary of the purpose of the experiment, as well as the method, results, and conclusion. For a simple experiment your abstract may only be a few lines; even for a complex one, you should keep it to about two hundred words.

Introduction

The introduction should give a more detailed statement of your purpose or objective. If, as is often the case, the purpose is to test a hypothesis arising from a specific problem, you should clearly and explicitly state the nature of both the problem and the hypothesis. Your introduction should include the theory underlying the experiment and any pertinent background data or equations. Although you may refer to papers relevant to the experiment, it's best to avoid quoting extensively.

Materials

This section should provide a list of the materials and equipment used and some explanation of how the experiment is set up. If different arrangements of equipment are required, give a full list of the equipment in this section, and then in the *Method* section describe each separate arrangement before you describe the respective tests. When the description of the materials is short, you may combine this section with the *Method* section. Many departments encourage students in first- and second-year courses to have a single *Materials and Method* section.

A simple diagram will help the reader to visualize the arrangement of equipment. If the diagram is too large to fit a regular page, you can draw it on an appropriately labelled attachment at the back of the report, and refer to it within the body of the report.

Note that some departments require that you specify the source or supplier of any reagents you have used. Such information should be included in this section: for example, ''Spectroscopic grade carbon tetrachloride (99% pure) was obtained from B.D.H. Chemicals.''

Method

This section is a step-by-step description of the procedures in the order in which you actually performed them. It must be written with enough detail that others will have no difficulty in repeating the experiment. If you are following instructions in a lab manual, you may not need to copy them out word for word; simply refer to the instructions and give details of any deviation. When a certain procedure is long, complicated, or not necessary to a full understanding of the experiment, you may describe it in a labelled attachment at the end of the report.

If you have undertaken a number of tests, you should begin with a short summary statement listing and numbering the tests so that the reader will be prepared for the series. To avoid confusion you should describe the tests in the same order in which you have listed them, giving them the same numbers and subheadings.

Although you should be concise in your description of the experimental method, make sure that you don't omit essential details. If you heated a test tube, for example, you must report at what temperature it was heated and for how long. If you performed a chromatography or other process at a faster or slower rate than usual, you must state the rate. Readers must know exactly what controls to apply if they try to perform the experiment themselves.

You should describe your experiments in the past tense. When you want to give instructions rather than a description of your method, use the imperative: for example, "Cut off 1 cm from the bottom of the stem."

Scientists writing for scientific journals are divided as to whether you should use the active or passive voice. Most prefer to use the passive voice ("The beaker was heated," rather than "I heated the beaker") because they believe that its impersonal quality helps to maintain the detached, clinical tone appropriate to a scientific report. Nevertheless, some scientists have recently begun using the active voice ("I heated the beaker") because it is clearer and less likely to lead to awkward, convoluted sentences. Ask your instructor about the department's preferences. Whichever voice you use, remember to strive for both clarity and objectivity.

Results

In this section you should report your observations, data, and calculations. Find out from your instructor whether you are expected to give the details of your calculations or only the results of those calculations. In either case, you should pay special attention to the units of any quantities: to omit or misuse them is a serious scientific mistake. Taking care to include all units will also reveal mistakes in your calculations that might otherwise go undetected. If your units don't cancel properly to yield the result you expect, you will know that you have made an error.

You should also make sure where possible that the calculated values you report include the "uncertainty" in each of them. For example, you might report that the calculated volume of a hollow sphere is 23.45 $\pm$ .05 cc (where $\pm$ .05 is the uncertainty in the volume measurement). When reporting any calculations or measurements, check to see if you need to include the standard deviation, the standard error of the mean, or the coefficient of variation.

The format of the *Results* section depends on the type of experiment performed. Whenever possible, summarize your results on a graph or table. A graph (or chart) is usually preferable to a table since it has more impact, but if you have made several measurements you are probably best to report in tabular form. When devising a graph remember these rules:

- use properly ruled graph paper;
- use a scale that will allow you to distribute your data points as widely as possible on the page;
- put error bars ($\pm$) on data points, where possible;
- label the axes, including the units used, so that the reader knows exactly what you have plotted on the graph;
- title the graph and label it (for example, ''Figure 1''), so that you can refer to it by number in your report.

Discussion

This part of the lab report allows you the greatest freedom, since your purpose is to examine and interpret the test results and to comment on their significance. You want to show how the test produced its outcome, whether expected or unexpected, and to discuss those elements that influenced the results. In determining what details to include in the analysis section, you might try to answer the following questions:

- Do the results reflect the objective of the experiment?
- Did the experimental method help you to accomplish the purpose of the test?
- Do the results obtained agree with previous results as reported in the literature on the subject? If not, how can you account for the discrepancy between accepted values and those you have found experimentally? What (if anything) probably went wrong during your experiment, and why? What was the source of any error?
- Can the results have another explanation?

For a good discussion, remember to think critically not only about your own work, but about how it relates to previous work.

Conclusion

This is a simple statement of the experiment's conclusion. You don't necessarily need a separate section; the conclusion can also appear as a short summary at the end of the *Discussion* section. You may include a table if you think that a graphic presentation will clarify the conclusion.

References

You should list the sources of any information used in your report. If you need to acknowledge a number of sources, you may list them in separate categories, such as *Books* and *Journals*. For details on the correct form for scientific documentation, see Chapter 11.

REPORT-WRITING STYLE

Scientific reports, like essays, must be written with the reader in mind. Since your reader is your instructor, you don't need to define elementary terms or explain a method that would be taken for granted by anyone with scientific training. At the same time, you should avoid filling your report with technical jargon when non-technical language will suit just as well. The watchwords are clarity and precision; you want to make it easy for the reader to understand exactly what you mean.

Although the basic rules are the same as for any other kind of writing, scientific reports do pose special problems for students. Here are a few words of advice:

Avoid using too many nouns as adjectives

Clusters of nouns used as adjectives can create cumbersome phrases:

orig. Adult male kidney disease
rev. Kidney disease in adult males

orig. Apparatus construction
rev. Construction of apparatus

Of course, some nouns are frequently and quite acceptably used as adjectives: for example, *kidney* disease, *hydrogen* bomb, *reaction* time, *S.I.* units. Your ear is probably the best judge of what is awkward and what is not.

Avoid using too many abstract nouns

Whenever possible, choose a verb rather than an abstract noun:

orig. The <u>addition</u> of acid and subsequent <u>agitation</u> of the solution resulted in the <u>formation</u> of crystals.

rev. When acid <u>was added</u> and the solution <u>shaken</u>, crystals <u>formed</u>.

rev. When I <u>added</u> acid to the solution and <u>shook</u> it, crystals <u>formed</u>.

Avoid vague qualifiers

As a scientist you must be exact. In particular, you should avoid words such as *quite*, *very*, *fairly*, *some*, or *many*, when you can use a more exact term. *Relatively* is especially dangerous unless you are actually relating two or more things.

Avoid unnecessary passive constructions

Although you may prefer to use passive verbs for describing methods and results, you should try to use active verbs in your *Introduction*, *Discussion*, and *Conclusion* sections. Your sentences will be clearer and more direct:

orig · pH4 <u>is needed</u> for the enzyme.
rev. The enzyme <u>needs</u> pH4.

orig · It <u>was reported</u> by E.A. Robinson . . .
rev. E.A. Robinson <u>reported</u> . . .

Avoid ambiguous pronouns

A pronoun will cause confusion if the reader can't tell which noun it refers to:

> To germinate, the seed requires water. <u>It</u> must be warm.

Is it the seed or the water that must be warm? If there is any chance of ambiguity, you should repeat the noun:

> The <u>water</u> must be warm.
> (or)
> The <u>seed</u> must be warm.

Be especially careful that the pronoun *this* clearly refers to a specific noun:

orig · When removed from the water, the stalk lost its leaves. <u>This</u> occurred over eight hours.

rev. When removed from the water, the stalk lost its leaves. <u>This loss</u> occurred over eight hours.

5
WRITING
a business report

In many business courses you will have to write the kind of formal report used in the business world. This chapter shows you how to do it. Details will depend on the circumstances, but these guidelines will give you the general strategies and techniques for effective report-writing, whether in school or on the job. Remember that course reports are usually hypothetical exercises designed to see if you understand the process of writing an actual report.

PLANNING THE REPORT

First principles

Business managers with many demands on their time want to know the central idea of a report as quickly as possible. They also want to trust in its accuracy. When writing a business report, therefore, try to follow three basic principles:

1. Put the most important information up front, unless you have a particular reason to do otherwise. In fact, in most cases it's a good idea to put the essence of what you want to say in your first page or so, just in case that's all your reader happens to read.
2. Be concise. A report should say as much as possible in as little space as possible.
3. Be objective. Readers must be confident that the information you are providing is free of personal biases. Logical analysis will make your work believable (for more details, see p. 42).

Defining the task: the four R's

A business report that is off-target or of little interest to the reader is more likely to be filed than acted on. To create a focused and interesting report, you need to plan carefully. As in any other kind of writing, the time you spend organizing your thoughts and devising your strategies is well worth the effort. The first step is to define precisely what it is that you have to do. Before you even begin to write, examine the task by asking questions about four aspects: Reason, Reader, Restrictions, and Research. (Don't forget that for course work, you must define the task as if it were the real thing.)

1. What is the reason?

Why are you writing this report? What goal is it supposed to achieve? Broadly speaking, every report has one of two basic purposes: either to provide information, or to recommend some course of action. Many informational reports such as progress, production, or monthly sales reports are used regularly to pass along facts as they accumulate; unless they focus on exceptional rather than routine matters, such reports tend to be treated as a kind of bureaucratic busy work. On the other hand, reports that are written to fill specific needs—to help someone make a decision, or to suggest a solution to a particular problem— usually receive close attention from both writer and reader. Examples would be suggestions for a new product line, a feasibility study on a proposed plant location, or recommendations for reversing a sales decline. Fortunately, this is the kind of challenging report you will be asked to write for most courses. It provides the most opportunity for you as the writer to show your ability to make inferences and judgements—both marks of managerial competence.

Determining the reason for such a report means establishing both its purpose and its expected outcome. If an important decision rests on your report, you will have to consider exactly what information is needed to make that decision, and precisely how you will support any recommendations.

2. Who is the reader?

Although a non-routine report may be read by several people, it is usually directed to one primary reader. Identifying your reader will enable you to organize and present your material in such a way that it's likely to be well received. (Your instructors will analyse your work from the relevant business perspective.) Among the details you should consider are the following:

What type of person is the reader? Often the reaction will depend less on the nature of the reader's job than on his or her personality. A cautious, conservative person might favour a carefully understated position, whereas a bold, creative type might prefer a more daring or imaginative approach. If your personal knowledge of the reader is slight, you can probably find someone reliable to give you a few clues.

What is the relationship? Is the reader your boss, or a colleague? How has he or she reacted to past communications with you? If you are writing for someone in a position far up the line from you, your tone and approach will probably be more formal than they would be for someone you talk to often.

Has the reader asked for the report? If you are writing in response to a request, you may not need to fill in much detail about the purpose, but if the report is unsolicited you should take care to place it in a context.

What is the reader's field of interest or responsibility? You will need to go into more detail about an area that is your reader's speciality than you will for one in which he or she is less interested. Usually top management will want an overview, whereas a specialist will require all the particulars.

In the business world your report might be going to several different kinds of readers—to a plant supervisor, say, as well as to top management. If so, you could consider giving the complete analysis to the supervisor, and sending top management only an executive summary.

How is the reader likely to respond to the report? If you can anticipate probable objections or concerns and answer them in the report itself, your work will be that much more convincing.

How might the reader benefit from the report? Your suggestions will be more persuasive if you can point out their advantages for the reader. The benefit could be significant: giving the reader a competitive edge in the marketplace, for example, or saving the business itself from impending financial collapse. Even if the benefit is a more general one, such as improving the reader's ability to anticipate future problems, you should point it out.

3. What are the restrictions?

From the outset, you will have to consider the practical restrictions on your writing. How much time do you have? How much help is available for typing the report and for producing illustrations, photographs, or models?

Other kinds of restriction will apply to the subject of the report. Since it's always better to do a thorough job on a narrow subject than a superficial job on a broad one, you must limit your topic to manageable proportions. If you are doing a report on newspaper readership, for example, you could consider restricting it by time (a specific year or years), by geography (a certain region or market), or by kind (daily or weekly papers). If you are writing a report on office computers, you might want to limit it to micro-computers, or to those in a certain price range. At the same time you should take into account the reader's perspective. For instance, it would be an annoying waste of his or her time if you were to include any computers that were too expensive even to consider. Careful restriction of the topic will spare your reader the trouble of going through unnecessary material.

4. What research is required?

In deciding what information to gather, you should weigh the time and money required to do the research against its usefulness to the report. In other words, you must determine what is essential.

Research decisions will be easier if you work out your topic in precise terms. A topic such as ''A Report on Computers'' is too vague to be useful; it will be much more helpful if you can be specific: ''A Cost-Benefit Analysis of Three Micro-Computers for Use in the Accounting Department of Dominion Appliances.'' You should then consider research needs in relation to the first three R's: Reason, Reader, and Restrictions.

It's especially useful to determine how much your readers already know; many will need no background information at all. If you must provide some, remember that too much detail will draw attention away from more important matters. (One solution would be to attach a short background section as an appendix at the end of the report.)

Once you have decided on the information you need, you should ask yourself what, if anything, you have to verify. Is your source reliable? Should you cross-check any facts or figures? Remember that a source with a special interest in the matter may either exaggerate or gloss over certain aspects. Statistics themselves may not lie, but they can easily distort the picture.

Finally, you should determine the degree of accuracy or precision required for any figures you supply. Indicating the margin of error will show the reader that you are thorough and objective.

Often the facts and figures you need can be obtained internally, either by questioning people on the job or by researching company documents. If you find that an earlier report covers some of the same ground you are working on, you could well refer to it and make use of what you need, up-dating as necessary. If wider research is required, you will find librarians helpful in locating relevant government documents, company reports, or academic studies. (Of course, when you use another person's material you must acknowledge it and give proper references: see Chapter 10.)

When you have to obtain your own data—through a questionnaire or survey, for example—make sure that any statistical results are based on an appropriate sample. If you aren't familiar with proper sampling methods yourself, consult someone who is: nothing will weaken your credibility more than providing unreliable or invalid statistical information. Research information is only valuable if it is accurate.

Organizing your information

The next step is to decide on the most effective way of organizing the information you have gathered. The order will depend on both the nature of the report and the anticipated response of the reader to any recommendations you make. You can follow either of two basic approaches:

1. The direct (deductive) approach

This is the most common order. Use it if your report is the routine informational kind or if you expect the reader to respond favourably. The most important information (usually the recommendations or conclusions) comes first and the least important information (supporting material) last:

1. Recommendations (Conclusions)
2. Purpose
3. Method
4. Findings

2. The indirect (inductive) approach

This approach is useful if you think that your reader's initial response to your conclusions or recommendations will be unfavourable. Rather than emphasizing your conclusions right away, you lead into them gradually, showing in a careful, step-by-step way how you reached them. If your logic and research are sound, the reader should find your conclusions inevitable. Here is the basic order:

1. Purpose
2. Method
3. Findings
4. Recommendations (Conclusions)

Sometimes a long formal report will follow this order, but in effect change the format to a direct one by beginning with a summary that condenses the recommendations or conclusions:

1. Summary of Recommendations (Conclusions)
2. Purpose
3. Method
4. Findings
5. Recommendations (Conclusions)

In fact, a summary is often a benefit in a long report, even if you are following the usual direct order, because it provides a busy reader with a brief outline of your conclusions and the reasoning behind them. If several people will be reading the report, you can give the summary to those who want a general overview and the full report to interested experts.

Organizing the details

The principle of "important things first" also applies to the arrangement of points within each section. In the *Recommendations* section especially, it's a good idea to put your most important point at the beginning and give the rest in descending order of importance. If you are trying to persuade a hostile or skeptical reader, however, you might be wise to begin with the point, major or minor, that will get the most favourable reaction.

The *Findings* section, usually the most detailed part of a report, may require a different approach, especially if it is long. When you have a lot of material to cover, you should try to let your purpose determine the way you arrange it:

- to present a job description, you could divide the information into classes or parts;

- to describe a process, you could present the stages in chronological order;
- to discuss the different markets for a product, you could arrange your findings according to geographical regions.

Ordering for comparison

When you are presenting information from which a choice will be made, you should order it in such a way that the reader will be able to compare the options easily. For example, suppose that you have been asked to suggest a micro-computer for an office and are considering three models: Computer X, Computer Y, and Computer Z. Rather than presenting the strengths and weaknesses of each in turn, decide on the criteria for comparison, and then for each criterion compare all three models. With four criteria—memory capacity, software, cost, and expandability—the plan for your *Findings* section might look like this:

A. Computer X has the best memory capacity.
 1. Computer X
 2. Computer Y
 3. Computer Z

B. Computer X has the widest range of software.
 1. Computer X
 2. Computer Y
 3. Computer Z

C. Computer Z is the least expensive.
 1. Computer X
 2. Computer Y
 3. Computer Z

D. Computer X is the most expandable.
 1. Computer X
 2. Computer Y
 3. Computer Z

Whichever way you choose to order the details, remember to be systematic and consistent. In addition, it's a good idea to include a chart, table or matrix to illustrate visually the points of comparison (see pp. 44-7).

Beginnings

An internal office report may require nothing more than a memo heading. For more formal reports, however, you will have to supply some or all of the following:

Title page. The title you choose should be as precise and descriptive as possible: not just "Feasibility Study: Plant Location," for example, but "A Comparison of Possible Central Ontario Locations for the Monarch Auto Parts Plant." The title page should also indicate who requested the report, who wrote it, and the date of presentation:

> Prepared for Arthur Jones, President
> Monarch Industries Ltd.
>
> by
>
> Michelle Smart
> Ace Consultants
>
> June 10, 1983

(For a course assignment, don't forget to include the necessary academic information, such as course name or number.)

Table of contents. A table of contents is helpful in a long report because it allows the reader to find specific information quickly. Formats may vary. To be clear, however, you should number the sections according to their numbering in the report, and indent subheadings. Place page numbers in a corresponding column at the right-hand side of the page.

Letter of transmittal. This is a personal letter to the intended reader. It may be attached to the front of the report or placed after the title page. The letter usually opens with a sentence on the subject of the report, then moves on to a short review. (If the report includes a summary, this review should be very brief; on the other hand, the review may replace the summary altogether, by stating the report's conclusions or recommendations.) The letter of transmittal may also be used to acknowledge anyone who has helped in preparing the report. In closing, you might thank the reader for giving you this chance to contribute, or express your hope for another such opportunity in the future. (A letter of transmittal is usually not required for course assignments.)

Endings

After the main body of your report, you may include one or both of the following:

Appendix. An appendix contains any material that provides a useful backup but is not essential to the report. It might include tables, figures, or graphs; the questionnaire used in a survey; summaries of raw data; parts of other reports that are pertinent to your findings; or any other information that would slow the reader down unnecessarily if it appeared in the main text.

Bibliography. This should include any documents, published or unpublished, used in preparing the report. Items should be listed in alphabetical order. The format usually follows that given in Chapter 10, but it may vary depending on the business context. If you have made specific references to outside sources, you should also provide footnotes; in business reports these are usually placed at the end of the text rather than at the bottom of the page.

WRITING THE REPORT

Like any other kind of writing, writing for business should be clear, concise, and forceful (see Chapter 7). Here are some additional guidelines especially useful for business reports:

1. Be objective

A business report must be as free as possible of biases and subjective opinions. Your reader will be more likely to accept your findings if you follow these suggestions:

Identify your assumptions. If you are comparing micro-computers, for example, and you assume that portability is not a factor, you should say so.

Avoid unsubstantiated judgements. Be sure that any suggestions you make or conclusions you reach follow from the information you have given. Never imply anything that you cannot prove. If your findings aren't fool-proof, show where the uncertainty lies.

Avoid subjective language. Words such as *terrible* or *fantastic* detract from the objective tone you want. Instead of saying "sales have shown an amazing increase," give the exact percentage of the increase and let the facts speak for themselves.

The overall tone to aim for depends on the circumstances—particularly the intended reader. If you are writing a short informal report to someone you often see, familiar terms such as *I* and *you* are appropriate, but many formal reports try to avoid the subjective impression created by personal pronouns. The result, unfortunately, is often a cumbersome load of passive constructions (see p. 65). Using an active construction and substituting *the author* or *the researcher* for *I* isn't the answer either. The best solution is to rethink the sentence and see if you can keep it active while avoiding the *I*'s:

orig. I found that Computer X had more options than the other models.

rev. Computer X has more options than the other models.

If you can't revise this way, you are better to use the odd *I* than to strangle your meaning in a convoluted *I*-less sentence.

2. Be specific

Although you don't have to give complete descriptive details for every fact you report, you should be as precise as possible when referring to people, places, times, and amounts—especially if you think the information might be disputed. Instead of saying

> Some time last month the president contacted the plant management and learned that some of the machines were not in operation,

say

> On May 25, Arthur Smith spoke to Len Jones, the plant manager, and learned that two of the punching machines had broken down.

Take care also to be specific in defining key terms. Precision is particularly important in the case of words such as *reliable*, which may have a special technical meaning to some people but a more general one to others. To avoid confusion you must make sure that your readers know exactly how you are using such terms.

Finally, remember that by being specific, you will make your writing not only more clear but more interesting as well: concrete language is lively language. (For more details, see p. 66.)

3. Use headings to tell the story

A report, unlike an essay, should use headings to distinguish the various sections. You may use a heading simply to indicate the topic of each section—for example, *Findings*—but it will be much more effective if it summarizes the most important point. Headings that "tell the story" enable the reader to find the key points in your report at a glance. As an example, see the outline for the microcomputer report (p. 40).

4. Number each section

Numbering helps to indicate each section's relative importance. Here are the three basic systems:

Roman numeral	Alphanumeric	Decimal
I.	A.	1.0
A.	1.	1.1
1.	a.	1.11
2.	b.	1.12
B.	2.	1.2
II.	B.	2.0

Most technical reports use the decimal system. Whichever method you choose, be sure to use equivalent symbols for sections of equivalent importance.

5. List information

Whenever you can simplify your material by listing it, do so; like a heading, a list is an aid to quick understanding. If you will be referring to the items in the list later, it's wise to number each one; otherwise you may simply use a dash (—) or a bullet (•).

6. Use visual aids

A visual aid such as a chart, matrix, or table is useful for presenting quantitative data. Charts come in three basic kinds; easier to grasp than tables, they are most suitable for comparing figures:

The line chart or graph shows change over a period of time; it's often used to point out trends or fluctuations in trends, as in a sales report:

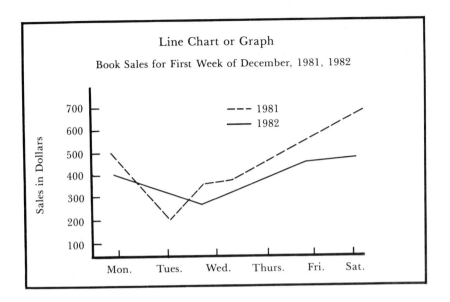

Line Chart or Graph

Book Sales for First Week of December, 1981, 1982

The bar chart is used to compare elements at a fixed point in time: for example, the comparative profits made by each company division:

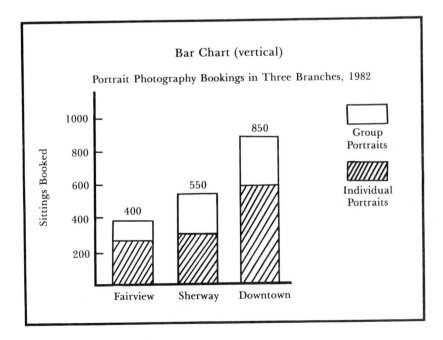

Bar Chart (vertical)

Portrait Photography Bookings in Three Branches, 1982

The pie chart is used to emphasize the proportions of individual items making up a whole: for example, the percentage of a company's total sales contributed by each department, or the individual expenses making up a department's total costs:

Pie Chart

Appliance Profits, 1981

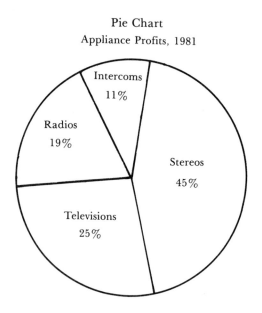

A matrix is another way of helping the reader to make comparisons, particularly of characteristics or qualitative information:

Matrix				
10-Day Vacation Packages to London				
Accommodation	Meals	Transportation	Extras	Cost
Plan 1 – Double (shared) with bath	——	8-day pass, London Transport	Bus tour to Oxford	$1050 each
Plan 2 – Double (shared)	Breakfast	——	——	$800 each
Plan 3 – Single with bath	Breakfast	——	Tickets to 3 plays	$1000 each

A table is useful when the reader needs to know a lot of precise figures; for example, the exact prices of certain items for each year in a five-year period:

Table

First Quarter Corporate Profits, 1981

Company	$ millions	Percentage change from 1980
Xenon Corp.	$5.6	+13%
Mayfair Industries	8.3	+10.2%
Dominion Consolidated	4.5	+1%
C.R.C. Ltd.	7.2	−1%

When using any of these visual aids, you must decide on the importance of the information it contains. If the information is supplementary, place it in an appendix; if it's essential, integrate it with the relevant discussion in the text. Wherever you place the aid, make sure you label and number it for easy reference, and check that all the parts are clearly identified.

7. Think about overall appearance

Remember that an effective report appeals to the eye as well as the mind. Here are a few suggestions:

- Generous use of space around the typescript will create a pleasing impression; wide margins and spaces between sections will help to break up an imposing mass of type.

- Individual headings and ideas will stand out better if you underline them or vary the typeface according to the importance of the heading.
- Changing the position of the headings to indicate the degree of importance will also make your report clearer visually.
- Primary headings should be fully capitalized and centred on the page; they may or may not be underlined.
- Secondary headings are usually underlined and placed by the left hand margin; you may capitalize the first letter of the first word, or of all important words.
- Third-level headings generally capitalize only the first letter; they are indented, underlined and placed on the same line as the following text:

PRIMARY HEADING

Secondary Heading
   Third-level heading. . . . (text material)

6
WRITING
an essay
examination

Most students feel nervous before examinations. It's not surprising. Writing an essay exam—even the open-book or take-home kind—imposes special pressures. Because the time is restricted, you can't edit and rewrite the way you can in a regular essay; because the questions are restricted, you must write on topics you might otherwise choose to avoid. You know that to do your best you need to feel calm—but how? These general guidelines will help you approach any essay exam with confidence; for special advice on open-book and take-home exams, see pp. 53-4.

GENERAL GUIDELINES

Before the exam

Review regularly

A weekly review of lecture notes and texts will help you not only to remember important material but to relate new information to old. If you don't review regularly, at the end of the year you'll be faced with relearning rather than remembering.

Set memory triggers

As you review, condense and focus the material by writing down in the margin key words or phrases that will trigger off a whole set of details in your mind. The trigger might be a concept word that names or points to an important theory or definition, or a quantitative phrase such as "three causes of the decline in manufacturing" or "five reasons for inflation."

Sometimes you can create an acronym or a nonsense sentence that will trigger an otherwise hard-to-remember set of facts—something like the acronym HOMES (Huron, Ontario, Michigan, Erie, Superior) for the Great Lakes. Since the difficulty of memorizing increases with the number of individual items you are trying to remember, any method that will reduce that number will increase your effectiveness.

Ask questions: try the three-C approach

Think of questions that will get to the heart of the material and cause you to examine the relations between various subjects or issues; then figure out how you would answer them. The three-C approach discussed on p. 7 may be a help. For example, reviewing the *components* of the subject could mean focusing on the main parts of an issue or on the definitions of major terms or theories. When reviewing *change* in the subject, you might ask yourself what elements caused it, directly or indirectly. To review *context* you might consider how certain aspects of the subject—issues, theories, actions, results—compare with others on the course. Essentially, what the three-C approach does is force you to look at the material from various perspectives.

Old examinations are useful both for seeing the type of question you might be asked and for checking on the thoroughness of your preparation. If old exams aren't available, you might get together with friends who are taking the same course and ask each other questions. Just remember that the most useful review questions are not the ones that require you to recall facts, but those that force you to analyse, integrate, or evaluate information.

Allow extra time

Give yourself lots of time to get to the exam. Nothing is more nerve-wracking than to think that you're going to be late. If you have to travel, don't forget that traffic can jam, and so can alarm clocks—remember Murphy's Law: "Whatever can go wrong will." Anticipate any unusual difficulties and allow yourself a good margin.

At the exam

Read the exam

An exam is not a hundred-metre dash; instead of starting to write immediately, take time at the beginning to read through each question and create a plan of action. A few minutes spent on thinking and organizing will bring better results than the same time spent on writing a few more lines.

Apportion your time

Reread the instructions carefully to find out how many questions you must answer and to see if you have any choice. Subtract five minutes or so for the initial planning, then divide the time you have left by the number of questions you have to answer. If possible, allow for a little extra time at the end to reread and edit your work. If the instructions on the exam indicate that not all questions are of equal value, apportion your time accordingly.

Choose your questions

Decide on the questions that you will do and the order in which you will do them. Your answers don't have to be in the same order as the questions. If you think you have lots of time, it's a good idea to place your best answer first, your worst answers in the middle, and your second best answer at the end, in order to leave the reader on a high note. If you think you will be rushed, though, it's wiser to work from best to worst. That way you will be sure to get all the marks you can on your good answers, and you won't have to cut a good answer short at the end.

Keep calm

If your first reaction on reading the exam is ''I can't do any of it!'' force yourself to keep calm; take ten slow, deep breaths as a deliberate relaxation exercise. Decide which is the question that you can answer best. Even if the exam seems disastrous at first, you can probably find one question that looks manageable: that's the one to begin with. It will get you rolling and increase your confidence. By the time you have finished, you are likely to find that your mind has worked through to the answer for another question.

Read each question carefully

As you turn to each question, read it again carefully and underline all the key words. The wording will probably suggest the number of parts your answer should have; be sure you don't overlook anything (a common mistake when people are nervous). Since the verb used in the question is usually a guide for the approach to take in your answer, it's especially important that you interpret the following terms correctly:

- *explain*: show the how's or why's;
- *compare*: give both similarities and differences—even if the question doesn't say *compare and contrast*;
- *outline*: state simply, without much development of each point (unless specifically asked);
- *discuss*: develop your points in an orderly way, taking into account contrary evidence or ideas.

Make notes

Before you even begin to organize your answer, jot down key ideas and information related to the topic on rough paper or the unlined pages of your answer book. These notes will save you the worry of forgetting something by the time you begin writing. Next, arrange those parts you want to use into a brief plan.

Be direct

Get to the points quickly and illustrate them frequently. In an exam, as opposed to a term paper, it's best to use a direct approach. Don't worry about composing a graceful introduction: simply state the main points that you are going to discuss, then get on with developing them. Remember that your paper will likely be one of many read and marked by someone who has to work quickly—the clearer your answers are, the better they will be received.

For each main point give the kind of specific details that will prove you really know the material. General statements will show you are able to assimilate information, but they need examples to back them up.

Write legibly

Writing that's hard to read produces a cranky reader. When the marker has to struggle to decipher your ideas, you may get poorer results than you deserve. If for some special reason (such as a physical handicap) your writing is hard to read, see if you can make special arrangements to use a typewriter. If your writing is just plain bad, it's probably better to print.

Write on alternate lines

Writing on every other line will not only make your writing easier to read, but leave you space for changes and additions; you won't have to cover your paper with a lot of messy circles and arrows.

Keep to your time plan

Keep to your plan and don't skip any questions. Try to write something on each topic. Remember that it's easier to score half marks for a question you don't know much about than it is to score full marks for one you could write pages on. If you find yourself running out of time on an answer and still haven't finished, summarize the remaining points and go on to the next question. Leave a large space between questions so that you can go back and add more if you have time. If you write a new ending, remember to cross out the old one—neatly.

Reread your answers

No matter how tired or fed up you are, reread your answers at the end, if there's time. Check especially for clarity of expression; try to get rid of confusing sentences and increase the logical connection between your ideas. Revisions that make answers easier to read are always worth the effort.

Writing an open-book exam

If you think that permission to take your books into the exam room is an ''Open Sesame'' to success, be forewarned. You could fall into the trap of relying too heavily on them; you may spend so much time rifling through pages and looking things up that you won't have time to write good answers. The result may be worse than if you had been allowed no books at all.

If you want to do well, use your books only to check information and look up specific, hard-to-remember details for a topic you already know a good deal about. For instance, if your subject is history you can look up exact dates or quotations; for a business subject you can look up some figures; for an English exam you can check the lines of a poem or the exact words of a character in a novel—if you know where to find them quickly. In other words, use the books to make sure your answers are precise and well illustrated. Never use them to replace studying and careful exam preparation.

Writing a take-home exam

The benefit of a take-home exam is that you have time to plan your answers and to consult your texts or other sources. The catch is that the time is usually less than it would be for an ordinary essay. Don't work yourself into a frenzy trying to respond with a polished research essay for each question; rather, use the extra time to create a well-written exam answer. Keep in mind that you were given this assignment to test your overall command of the course: your reader is likely to be less concerned with your specialized research than with evidence that you have understood and assimilated the material.

The guidelines for a take-home exam are therefore similar to those for a regular exam; the only difference is that you don't need to keep such a close eye on the clock:

1. Keep your introduction short and get to the point quickly.
2. Have a straightforward and obvious organizational pattern so that the reader can easily see your main ideas.
3. Use frequent concrete examples to back up your points.
4. Where possible, show the range of your knowledge of course material by referring to a number of different sources, rather than constantly using the same ones.
5. Try to show that you can analyse and evaluate material: that you can do more than simply repeat information.

7
WRITING
with style

Writing with style does not mean stuffing your prose with fancy words and extravagant images. Any style, from the simplest to the most elaborate, can be effective depending on the occasion and intent. Writers known for their style are those who have projected something of their own personality into their writing; we can hear a distinctive voice in what they say. Obviously it takes time to develop a unique style. To begin, you have to decide what general effect you want to create.

Taste in style reflects the times. In earlier centuries, when few people outside the leisured class ever had a chance to read, many respected writers wrote in an elaborate style that we would think much too wordy. Now almost all of us read, but newspapers, television, and radio compete with books for our attention, and as a result we tend to favour a simpler kind of writing. Journalists have led the trend towards short, easy-to-grasp sentences and paragraphs. Writing in an academic context, you may expect your audience to be more reflective than the average newspaper reader, but the most effective style is still one that is clear, concise, and forceful.

BE CLEAR

Since sentence structure is dealt with in Chapter 8, this section will focus on clear wording and paragraphing.

Choose clear words

A good dictionary is a wise investment; get into the habit of using one. It will give you not only common meanings, but less familiar applications, archaic uses, and derivations, as well as proper spelling.

Canadian usage and spelling may follow either British or American practices, but usually combine aspects of both; you should check before you buy a dictionary to be sure that it gives these variants.

A thesaurus lists words that are closely related in meaning. It can help when you want to avoid repeating yourself, or when you are fumbling for a word that's on the tip of your tongue. But be careful: make sure you remember the difference between denotative and connotative meanings. A word's denotation is its primary or "dictionary" meaning. Its connotations are any associations that it may suggest; they may not be as exact as the denotations, but they are part of the impression the word conveys. If you examine a list of "synonyms" in a thesaurus, you will see that even words with similar meanings can have dramatically different connotations. For example, alongside the word *indifferent* your thesaurus may give the following: *neutral, unconcerned, careless, easy-going, unambitious,* and *half-hearted.* Imagine the different impressions you would create if you chose one or the other of those words to complete this sentence: "Questioned about the experiment's chance of success, he was _____ in his response." In order to write clearly, you must remember that a reader may react to the suggestive meaning of a word as much as to its "dictionary" meaning.

Use plain English

Plain words are almost always more forceful than fancy ones. If you aren't sure what plain English is, think of everyday speech: how do you talk to your friends? Many of our most common words—the ones that sound most natural and direct—are short. A good number of them are also among the oldest words in the English language. By contrast, most of the words that English has derived from other languages are longer and more complicated; even after they've been used for centuries, they can still sound artificial. For this reason you should beware of words loaded with prefixes (*pre-, post-, anti-, pro-, sub-, maxi-,* etc.) and suffixes (*-ate, -ize, -tion,* etc.). These Latinate attachments can make individual words more precise and efficient, but putting a lot of them together will make your writing seem dense and hard to understand. In many cases you can substitute a plain word for a fancy one:

Fancy	*Plain*
determinant	cause
utilization	use

cognizant	aware
obviate	prevent
terminate	end
infuriate	anger
oration	speech
conclusion	end
requisite	needed
numerous	many
finalize	finish, complete
systematize	order
sanitize	clean
remuneration	pay
maximization	increase

Suggesting that you write in plain English does not mean that you should never pick an unfamiliar, long, or foreign word: sometimes those words are the only ones that will convey precisely what you mean. Inserting an unusual expression into a passage of plain writing can also be an effective means of catching the reader's attention—as long as you don't do it too often.

Be precise

Always be as precise or exact as you can. Avoid all-purpose adjectives like *major*, *significant*, and *important*, and vague verbs such as *involved, entail*, and *exist*, when you can be more specific:

orig. Donald Smith <u>was involved in</u> the construction of the CPR.

rev. Donald Smith <u>helped finance</u> the construction of the CPR.

Here's another example:

orig. Granting public-service employees the right to strike was a <u>significant</u> legacy of Lester Pearson's years as Prime Minister.

rev. Granting public-service employees the right to strike was a <u>costly</u> legacy of Lester Pearson's years as Prime Minister.

(or)

rev. Granting public-service employees the right to strike was a <u>beneficial</u> legacy of Lester Pearson's years as Prime Minister.

Avoid unnecessary qualifiers

Qualifiers such as *very*, *rather*, and *extremely* are over-used. Experienced writers know that saying something is *very beautiful* may have less impact than saying simply that it is *beautiful*. For example, compare these sentences:

> That is a beautiful garden.

> That is a very beautiful garden.

Which has more punch?

When you think that an adjective needs qualifying—and sometimes it will—first see if it's possible to change either the adjective or the phrasing. Instead of writing

> Imperial Castings made a very big profit last year.

write

> Imperial Castings made an unprecedented profit last year.

or (if you aren't sure whether or not the profit actually set a record):

> Imperial Castings' profit rose forty per cent last year.

In some cases qualifiers not only weaken your writing but are redundant, since the adjectives themselves are absolutes. To say that something is *very unique* makes as much—or as little—sense as to say that someone is *rather pregnant* or *very dead*.

Avoid fancy jargon

All academic subjects have their own terminology; it may be unfamiliar to outsiders but it helps specialists to explain things to each other. The trouble is that people sometimes use jargon—special, technical language—unnecessarily, thinking it will make them seem more knowledgeable. Too often the result is not clarity, but complication. The guideline is easy: use specialized terminology only when it's a kind of shorthand that will help you explain something more precisely and efficiently. If plain prose will do just as well, stick to it.

Creating clear paragraphs

Paragraphs come in so many sizes and patterns that no single formula could possibly cover them all. The two basic principles to remember are these: (1) a paragraph is a means of developing and framing an idea or impression, and (2) the divisions between paragraphs aren't random, but indicate a shift in focus.

Develop your ideas

You are not likely to sit down and consciously ask yourself "What pattern shall I use to develop this paragraph? What comes first is the idea you intend to develop: the pattern the paragraph takes should flow from the idea itself and the way you want to discuss or expand it. (The most common ways of developing an idea are outlined on pp. 14-17.)

You may take one or several paragraphs to develop an idea fully. For a definition alone you could write one paragraph or ten, depending on the complexity of the subject and the nature of the assignment. Just remember that ideas need development, and that each new paragraph signals a change in idea.

Consider the topic sentence

Skilled skim-readers know that they can get the general drift of a book simply by reading the first sentence of each paragraph. The reason is that most paragraphs begin by stating the central idea to be developed. If you are writing your essay from a formal plan, you will probably find that each section and subsection will generate the topic sentence for a new paragraph.

Like the thesis statement for the essay as a whole, the topic sentence is not obligatory: in some paragraphs the controlling idea is not stated until the middle or even the end, and in others it is not stated at all but merely implied. Nevertheless, it's a good idea to think out a topic sentence for every paragraph. That way you'll be sure that each one has a readily graspable point and is clearly connected to what comes before and after. When revising your initial draft, check to see that each paragraph is held together by a topic sentence, either stated or implied. If you find that you can't formulate one, you should probably rework the whole paragraph.

Maintain focus

To be clear a paragraph should contain only those details that are in some way related to the central idea. It must also be structured so that the details are easily *seen* to be related. One way of showing these relations is to keep the same grammatical subject in most of the sentences that make up the paragraph. When the grammatical subject is shifting all the time, a paragraph loses focus, as in the following example:[1]

orig . <u>Boys</u> in school play a variety of sports these days. In the fall, <u>football</u> still attracts the most, although an increasing <u>number</u> now play soccer. For some <u>basketball</u> is the favourite when the ball season is over, but <u>you</u> will find that swimming or gymnastics are also popular. Cold winter <u>temperatures</u> may allow the school to have an outdoor rink, and then <u>hockey</u> becomes a source of enjoyment for many. In spring, though, the <u>rinks</u> begin melting, and so <u>there</u> is less opportunity to play. Then some <u>boys</u> take up soccer again, while track and field also attracts many participants.

Here the grammatical subject (underlined) is constantly jumping from one thing to another. Notice how much stronger the focus becomes when all the sentences have the same grammatical subject—either the same noun, a synonym, or a related pronoun:

new . <u>Boys</u> in school play a variety of sports these days. In the fall, <u>most</u> still choose football, although an increasing <u>number</u> now play soccer. When the ball season is over, <u>some</u> turn to basketball; <u>others</u> prefer swimming or gymnastics. If cold winter temperatures permit an outdoor rink, many <u>boys</u> enjoy hockey. Once the ice begins to melt in spring, though, <u>they</u> can play less often. Then <u>some</u> take up soccer again, while <u>others</u> choose track and field.

Naturally it's not always possible to retain the same grammatical subject throughout a paragraph. If you were comparing the athletic pursuits of boys and girls, for example, you would have to switch back and forth between boys and girls as your grammatical subject. In the same way, you will have to shift when you are discussing examples of an idea or exceptions to it.

Avoid monotony

If most or all of the sentences in your paragraph have the same grammatical subject, how do you avoid boring your reader? There are two easy ways:

Use stand-in words. Pronouns, either personal (*I, we, you, he, she, it, they*) or demonstrative (*this, that, those*) can stand in for the subject, as can synonyms (words or phrases that mean the same thing). The revised paragraph on boys' sports, for example, uses the pronouns *some, most,* and *they* as substitutes for *boys*. Most well-written paragraphs have a liberal sprinkling of these stand-in words.

"Bury" the subject by putting something in front of it. When the subject is placed in the middle of the sentence rather than at the beginning, it's less obvious to the reader. If you take another look at the revised paragraph, you'll see that in several sentences there is a word or phrase in front of the subject, giving the paragraph a feeling of variety. Even a single word, such as *first*, *then*, *lately*, or *moreover*, will do the trick. (Incidentally, this is a useful technique to remember when you are writing a letter of application and want to avoid starting every sentence with *I*.)

Link your ideas

To create coherent paragraphs, you need to link your ideas clearly. Linking words are those connectors—conjunctions and conjunctive adverbs—that show the *relations* between one sentence, or part of a sentence, and another; they're also known as transition words, because they bridge the transition from one thought to another. Make a habit of using linking words when you shift from one grammatical subject or idea to another, whether the shift occurs within a single paragraph or as you move from one paragraph to the next. Here are some of the most common connectors and the logical relations they indicate:

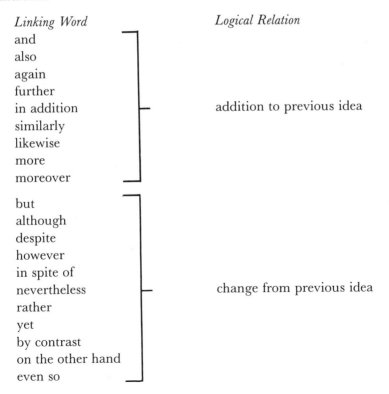

Linking Word	*Logical Relation*
and	
also	
again	
further	
in addition	addition to previous idea
similarly	
likewise	
more	
moreover	
but	
although	
despite	
however	
in spite of	
nevertheless	change from previous idea
rather	
yet	
by contrast	
on the other hand	
even so	

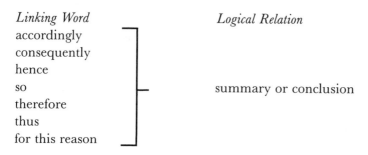

Linking Word

accordingly
consequently
hence
so
therefore
thus
for this reason

Logical Relation

summary or conclusion

Numerical terms such as *first*, *second*, and *third* also work well as links.

Vary the length, but avoid extremes

Ideally, academic writing will have a comfortable balance of long and short paragraphs. Avoid the extremes, especially the one-sentence paragraph, which can only state an idea, without explaining or developing it. A series of very short paragraphs is usually a sign that you have not developed your ideas in enough detail, or that you have started new paragraphs unnecessarily. On the other hand, a succession of long paragraphs can be tiring and difficult to read. In deciding when to start a new paragraph, remember always to consider what is clearest and most helpful for the reader.

BE CONCISE

At one time or another, you will probably be tempted to pad your writing. Whatever the reason—because you need to write two or three thousand words and have only enough to say for one thousand, or just because you think length is strength and hope to get a better mark for the extra—padding is a mistake. You may fool some of the people some of the time, but you are not likely to impress a first-rate mind with second-rate verbiage.

Strong writing is always concise. It leaves out anything that does not serve some communicative or stylistic purpose, in order to say as much as possible in as few words as possible. Concise writing will help you do better on both your essays and your exams.

Guidelines for concise writing

1. Use adverbs and adjectives sparingly

Avoid the shot-gun approach to adverbs and adjectives; don't just spray your work with modifiers in the hope that one will hit. One well-chosen word is always better than a series of synonyms:

orig. As well as being <u>costly</u> and <u>financially extravagant,</u> the venture is <u>reckless</u> and <u>foolhardy.</u>

rev. The venture is <u>foolhardy</u> as well as <u>costly.</u>

2. Avoid noun clusters

A recent trend in some writing is to use nouns as adjectives, as in the phrase *noun cluster*. This device can be effective occasionally, but frequent use can produce a monstrous pile-up of words. Breaking up noun clusters may not always produce fewer words, but it will make your writing easier to read:

orig. word-processor utilization manual
rev. manual for using word-processors

orig. pollution investigation committee
rev. committee to investigate pollution

3. Avoid chains of relative clauses

Sentences full of clauses beginning with *which*, *that*, or *who* are usually more wordy than necessary. Try reducing some of those clauses to phrases or single words:

orig. The solutions <u>which</u> were discussed last night have a practical benefit <u>which</u> is easily grasped by people <u>who</u> have no technical training.

rev. The solutions discussed last night have a practical benefit, easily grasped by non-technical people.

4. Try reducing clauses to phrases or words

Independent clauses can often be reduced by subordination. Here are a few examples:

orig. The report was written in a clear and concise manner and it was widely read.

rev. Written in a clear and concise manner, the report was widely read.

rev. Clear and concise, the report was widely read.

orig· His plan was of a radical nature and was a source of embarrassment to his employer.

rev. His radical plan embarrassed his employer.

For more detail on subordination and reduction, see p. 67.

5. Strike out hackneyed expressions and circumlocutions

Trite or roundabout phrases may flow from your pen without a thought, but they make for stale prose. Unnecessary words are deadwood; be prepared to hunt and chop ruthlessly to keep your writing vital:

Wordy	*Revised*
due to the fact that	because
at this point in time	now
consensus of opinion	consensus
in the near future	soon
when all is said and done	(omit)
in the eventuality that	if
in all likelihood	likely

6. Avoid "it is" and "there is" beginnings

Although it may not always be possible, try to avoid *it is* or *there is* (*are*) beginnings. Your sentences will be crisper and more concise:

orig· There is little time remaining for the sales manager to reverse the financial trend.

rev. Little time remains for the sales manager to reverse the financial trend.

orig· It is certain that pollution will increase.

rev. Pollution will certainly increase.

BE FORCEFUL

Developing a forceful, vigorous style simply means learning some common tricks of the trade and practising them until they become habit.

Choose active over passive verbs

An active verb creates more energy than a passive one does:

> Active: She threw the ball.

> Passive: The ball was thrown by her.

Moreover, passive constructions tend to produce awkward, convoluted phrasing. Writers of bureaucratic documents are among the worst offenders:

> It has been decided that the utilization of small rivers in the province for purposes of generating hydro-electric power should be studied by our department and that a report to the Deputy should be made by our Director as soon as possible.

The passive verbs in this mouthful make it hard to tell who is doing what.

Passive verbs are appropriate in two specific cases:

1. When the situation described is in fact passive—that is, when the subject of the sentence is the passive recipient of some action.
2. When using a passive verb will help to maintain focus by eliminating the need to shift to a different subject. The following example has both reasons for using the passive verb *were attacked*:

> The Jesuits began to convert the Hurons, but were attacked by an Iroquois band before they had completed the mission.

Use personal subjects

Most of us find it more interesting to learn about people than about things—hence the enduring appeal of the gossip columns. Wherever possible, therefore, make the subjects of your sentences personal. This trick goes hand-in-hand with use of active verbs. Almost any sentence becomes more lively with active verbs and a personal subject:

> orig. The outcome of the union members' vote was the decision to resume work on Monday.

> rev. The union members voted to return to work on Monday.

Here's another example:

> orig. It can be assumed that an agreement was reached, since there were smiles on both management and union sides when the meeting was finished.

rev. We can assume that <u>management and the union</u> <u>reached</u> <u>an agreement</u>, since <u>both bargainers</u> <u>were smiling</u> when <u>they</u> <u>finished</u> the meeting.

(or)

rev. Apparently <u>management and union</u> <u>reached</u> an agreement since, when <u>they</u> <u>finished</u> the meeting, <u>both bargainers</u> <u>were smiling</u>.

Use concrete details

Concrete details are easier to understand—and to remember—than abstract theories. Whenever you are discussing abstract concepts, therefore, always provide specific examples and illustrations; if you have a choice between a concrete word and an abstract one, choose the concrete. Consider this sentence:

> The French explored the northern territory and traded with the native people.

Now see how a few specific details can bring the facts to life:

> The French voyageurs paddled their way along the river systems of the north, trading their blankets and copper kettles for the Indians' furs.

Suggesting that you add concreteness doesn't mean getting rid of all abstractions. It's simply a plea to balance them with accurate details. Here is one instance in which added wording, if it is concrete and correct, can improve your writing.

Make important ideas stand out

Experienced writers know how to manipulate sentences in order to emphasize certain points. Here are some of their techniques:

Place key words in strategic positions

The positions of emphasis in a sentence are the beginning and, above all, the end. If you want to bring your point home with force, don't put the key words in the middle of the sentence. Save them for the last:

orig. People are less afraid of losing wealth than of losing face in this image-conscious society.

rev. In this image-conscious society, people are less afraid of losing wealth than of losing face.

Subordinate minor ideas

Small children connect incidents with a string of *and*s, as if everything were of equal importance:

> We went to the zoo and we saw a lion and John spilled his drink.

As they grow up, however, they learn to subordinate: that is, to make one part of a sentence less important in order to emphasize another point:

> Because the bus was delayed, we missed our class.

Major ideas stand out more and connections become clearer when minor ideas are subordinated:

orig. Night came and the ship slipped away from her captors.

rev. When night came, the ship slipped away from her captors.

Make your most important idea the subject of the main clause, and try to put it at the end, where it will be most emphatic:

orig. I was relieved when I saw my marks.

rev. When I saw my marks, I was relieved.

Vary sentence structure

As with anything else, variety adds spice to writing. One way of adding variety, which will also make an important idea stand out, is to use a periodic rather than a simple sentence structure.

Most sentences follow the simple pattern of subject—verb—object (plus modifiers):

> The <u>dog</u> <u>bit</u> the <u>man</u> on the ankle.
>   s   v   o

A *simple sentence* such as this gives the main idea at the beginning and therefore creates little tension. A *periodic sentence*, on the other hand, does not give the main clause until the end, following one or more subordinate clauses:

> Since he had failed to keep his promises or to inspire the voters, in the next election <u>he</u> <u>was defeated</u>.
>   s   v

The longer the periodic sentence is, the greater the suspense and the more emphatic the final part. Since this high-tension structure is more difficult to read than the simple sentence, your readers would be exhausted if you used it too often. Save it for those times when you want to create a special effect or play on emotions.

Vary sentence length

A short sentence can add punch to an important point, especially when it comes as a surprise. This technique can be particularly useful for conclusions. Don't overdo it, though. A string of long sentences may be monotonous, but a string of short ones has a staccato effect that can make your writing sound like a child's reader: "This is my dog. See him run."

Use contrast

Just as a jeweller will highlight a diamond by displaying it against dark velvet, so you can highlight an idea by placing it against a contrasting background:

orig. Most employees in industry do not have indexed pensions.

rev. Unlike civil servants, most employees in industry do not have indexed pensions.

Using parallel phrasing will increase the effect of the contrast:

> Although he often spoke to business groups, he seldom spoke in Parliament.

Use a well-placed adverb or correlative construction

Adding an adverb or two can sometimes help you to dramatize a concept:

orig. Although I dislike the proposal, I must accept it as the practical answer.

rev. Athough <u>emotionally</u> I dislike the concept, <u>intellectually</u> I must accept it as the practical answer.

Correlatives such as *both . . . and* or *not only . . . but also* can be used to emphasize combinations as well:

orig. Smith was a good coach and a good friend.

rev. Smith was <u>both</u> a good coach <u>and</u> a good friend.

rev. Smith was <u>not only</u> a good coach <u>but also</u> a good friend.

Use repetition

Repetition is a highly effective emphatic device. It helps to stir the emotions:

> He fought injustice and corruption. He fought complacent politicians and inept policies. He fought hard, but he always fought fairly.

Of course, you would only use such a dramatic technique on rare occasions.

Use your ears

Your ears are probably your best critics: make good use of them. Before producing a final copy of any piece of writing, read it out loud, in a clear voice. The difference between cumbersome and fluent passages will be unmistakable.

Some final advice: write before you revise

No one would expect you to sit down and put all this advice into practice as soon as you start to write. You would feel so constrained that it would be hard to get anything down on paper at all. You will be better off if you begin practising these techniques during the editing process, when you are looking critically at what you have already written. Some experienced writers can combine the creative and critical functions, but most of us find it easier to write a rough draft first, before starting the detailed task of revising.

NOTE

[1]Discussion of focus and examples based on Robert Cluett and Lee Ahlborn, *Effective English Prose* (New York: L.W. Singer Co., 1965), 51.

8
COMMON ERRORS
in grammar and
usage

This chapter is not a comprehensive grammar lesson: it's simply a survey of those areas where students most often make mistakes. It will help you to keep a look-out for weaknesses as you are editing your work. Once you get into the habit of checking, it won't be long before you are correcting potential problems as you write.

The grammatical terms used here are the most simple and familiar ones; if you need to review some of them, see the Glossary. For a thorough treatment of grammar or usage, consult a complete text such as A.J. Thompson and A.V. Martinet's *A Practical English Grammar*, 3rd ed. (Oxford: Oxford University Press, 1980).

Troubles with sentence unity

Sentence fragments

To be complete, a sentence must have both a subject and a verb in an independent clause; if it doesn't, it's a fragment. Occasionally a sentence fragment is acceptable, as in

✓ Will the government try to abolish the Senate? <u>Not likely.</u>

Here the sentence fragment *not likely* is clearly intended to be understood as a short form of *It is not likely that it will try*. Unintentional sentence fragments, on the other hand, usually seem incomplete rather than shortened:

✗ I enjoy living in Vancouver. <u>Being a skier who likes the sea.</u>

The last ''sentence'' is incomplete: where is the subject or verb? (Remember that a participle such as *being* is a verbal, not a verb.) The fragment can be made into a complete sentence by adding a subject and a verb:

✓ I am a skier who likes the sea.

Alternatively, you could join the fragment to the preceding sentence:

✓ Being a skier who likes the sea, I enjoy living in Vancouver.

✓ I enjoy living in Vancouver, since I am a skier who likes the sea.

Run-on sentences

A run-on sentence is one that continues beyond the point where it should have stopped:

✗ Mosquitoes and blackflies are annoying, but they don't stop tourists from coming to spend their holidays in Canada and such is the case in Ontario's northland.

The *and* should be dropped and a period or semicolon added after *Canada*.

Another kind of run-on sentence is one in which two independent clauses (phrases that could stand by themselves as sentences) are wrongly joined by a comma:

✗ Northrop Frye has won international acclaim as a critic, he is an English professor at the University of Toronto.

This error is known as a *comma splice*. There are three ways of correcting it:

• by putting a period after *critics* and starting a new sentence:

✓ . . . as a critic. He . . .

• by replacing the comma with a semicolon:

✓ . . . as a critic; he . . .

• by making one of the independent clauses subordinate to the other:

✓ Northrop Frye, who has won international acclaim as a critic, is an English professor at the University of Toronto.

The one exception to the rule that independent clauses cannot be joined by a comma arises when the clauses are very short and arranged in a tight sequence:

✓ I opened the door, I saw the skunk, I shut the door.

Such instances are obviously uncommon.

Contrary to what many people think, words such as *however, therefore,* and *thus* cannot be used to join independent clauses:

✗ Two of my friends started out in Commerce, however they quickly decided they didn't like accounting.

The mistake can be corrected by beginning a new sentence after *Commerce* or (preferably) by putting a semicolon in the same place:

✓ Two of my friends started out in Commerce; however, they quickly decided they didn't like accounting.

The only words that can be used to join independent clauses are the coordinating conjunctions—*and, or, nor, but, for, yet,* and *so*—and subordinating conjunctions such as *if, because, since, while, when, where, after, before,* and *until.*

Faulty predication

When the subject of a sentence is not grammatically connected to what follows (the predicate), the result is *faulty predication*:

✗ The <u>reason</u> for his downfall was <u>because</u> he couldn't handle people.

The problem is that *because* essentially means the same thing as *the reason for.* The subject needs a noun clause to complete it:

✓ The <u>reason</u> for his downfall was <u>that</u> he couldn't handle people.

Another solution would be to rephrase the sentence:

✓ He was defeated because he couldn't handle people.

Faulty *is when* or *is where* constructions can be corrected in the same way:

✗ The difficulty <u>is when</u> the two sides disagree.

✓ The difficulty <u>arises when</u> the two sides disagree.

Troubles with subject-verb agreement

Identifying the subject

A verb should always agree in number with its subject. Sometimes, however, when the subject does not come at the beginning of the sentence, or when it is separated from the verb by other information, you may be tempted to use a verb form that does not agree:

X The increase in the rate for freight and passengers were condemned by the farmers.

The subject here is *increase*, not *freight and passengers*; therefore the verb should be the singular *was condemned*:

✓ The increase in the rate for freight and passengers was condemned by the farmers.

Either, neither, each

The indefinite pronouns *either*, *neither*, and *each* always take singular verbs:

X Neither of the changing rooms have a sauna.

✓ Each of them has a shower.

Compound subjects

When *or*, *either . . . or*, or *neither . . . nor* is used to create a compound subject, the verb should usually agree with the last item in the subject:

✓ Neither my room-mate nor my team-mates are going home for the holiday.

If a singular item follows a plural item, however, a singular verb may sound awkward, and it's better to rephrase the sentence:

orig . Either my history books or my biology text is going to gather dust this weekend.

new . This weekend, I'm going to leave behind either my history books or my biology text.

Unlike the word *and*, which creates a compound subject and therefore takes a plural verb, *as well as* or *in addition to* does not create a compound subject; therefore the verb remains singular:

✓ Tourtière and sugar-pie are traditional French-Canadian dishes.

✓ Tourtière <u>as well as</u> sugar-pie <u>is</u> a traditional French-Canadian dish.

Collective nouns

A collective noun is a singular noun, such as *family*, *army*, or *team*, that includes a number of members. If the noun refers to the members as a unit, it takes a singular verb:

✓ The <u>family goes</u> on holiday in June.

If the noun refers to the members as individuals, however, the verb becomes plural:

✓ The <u>team</u> <u>are receiving</u> their sweaters before the exhibition game.

✓ The <u>majority</u> of immigrants to Canada <u>settle</u> in cities.

Titles

A title is singular even if it contains plural words; therefore it takes a singular verb:

✓ <u>Tales of the South Pacific</u> was a best-seller.

✓ McCarthy and McCarthy is handling the case.

Tense troubles

Native speakers of English usually know the correct sequence of verb tense by ear, but a few tenses can still be confusing.

The past perfect

If the main verb is in the past tense and you want to refer to something before that time, use the past perfect (*had* plus the past participle). The time sequence will not be clear if you use the simple past in both clauses:

X   He hoped that she <u>bought</u> the typewriter.

✓ He hoped that she <u>had bought</u> the typewriter.

Similarly, when you are reporting what someone said in the past—that is, when you are using past indirect discourse—you should use the past perfect tense in the clause describing what was said:

X   He said that the party <u>caused</u> the neighbours to complain.

✓ He said that the party <u>had caused</u> the neighbours to complain.

Using "if"

When you are describing a possibility in the future, use the present tense in the condition (*if*) clause and the future tense in the consequence clause:

✓ If he <u>tests</u> us on French verbs, I <u>will fail</u>.

When the possibility is unlikely, it is conventional—especially in formal writing—to use the subjunctive in the *if* clause, and *would* plus the base verb in the consequence clause:

✓ If he <u>were to cancel</u> the test, I <u>would cheer</u>.

When you are describing a hypothetical instance in the past, use the past subjunctive (it has the same form as the past perfect) in the *if* clause and *would have* plus the past participle for the consequence. A common error is to use *would have* in both clauses:

✗ If she <u>would have been</u> more friendly, I <u>would have asked</u> her to dance.

✓ If she <u>had been</u> more friendly, I <u>would have asked</u> her to dance.

Writing about literature

When you are describing a literary work in its historical context, use the past tense:

✓ Margaret Atwood <u>wrote</u> <u>Surfacing</u> at a time when George Grant's <u>Technology and Empire</u> <u>was persuading</u> people to reassess technocratic values.

To discuss what goes on *within* a work of literature, however, you should use the present tense:

✓ The narrator <u>retreats</u> to the woods and <u>tries</u> to escape the rationalism of her father's world.

When you are discussing an episode or incident in a literary work and want to refer to a prior incident or a future one, use past or future tenses accordingly:

✓ The narrator returns to northern Quebec, where she <u>spent</u> her summers as a child; by the time she leaves, she <u>will have rediscovered</u> herself.

Be sure to return to the present tense when you have finished referring to events in the past or future.

Pronoun troubles

Pronoun reference

The link between a pronoun and the noun it refers to must be clear. If the noun doesn't appear in the same sentence as the pronoun, it should appear in the preceding sentence:

X   The textbook supply in the bookstore had run out, and so we borrowed <u>them</u> from the library.

Since *textbook* is used as an adjective rather than a noun, it cannot serve as referent or antecedent for the pronoun *them*. You must either replace *them* or change the phrase *textbook supply*.

✓   The <u>textbook supply</u> in the bookstore had run out, and so we borrowed the <u>texts</u> from the library.

✓   The <u>textbooks</u> in the bookstore had run out, and so we borrowed <u>them</u> from the library.

When a sentence contains more than one noun, make sure there is no ambiguity about which noun the pronoun refers to:

X   The public wants increased social <u>services</u> as well as lower <u>taxes</u>, but the government does not advocate <u>them</u>.

What does the pronoun *them* refer to? The taxes, the social services, or both?

✓   The public wants <u>increased</u> social <u>services</u> as well as lower taxes, but the government does not advocate such <u>increases</u>.

Using "it" and "this"

Using *it* and *this* without a clear referent can lead to confusion:

X   Although the directors wanted to meet in January, <u>it</u> (this) didn't take place until May.

✓   Although the directors wanted to meet in January, <u>the conference</u> didn't take place until May.

Make sure that *it* or *this* clearly refers to a specific noun or pronoun.

Pronoun agreement

A pronoun should agree in number and person with the noun that it refers to:

X When a Canadian civil <u>servant</u> retires, <u>their</u> pension is indexed.

✓ When a Canadian civil <u>servant</u> retires, <u>his</u> pension is indexed.

Traditionally, the word *his* has been used to indicate both male and female, and most grammarians still maintain that *his* is the correct form. If you feel uncomfortable about using *his* alone, or want to avoid charges of sexism, now and again you may resort to the more cumbersome *his or her*, as this handbook occasionally does. Where possible, though, it's better to try switching from the singular to the plural in both noun and pronoun:

✓ When Canadian civil <u>servants</u> retire, <u>their pensions</u> are indexed.

Whichever form you choose, check for agreement.

Using "one"

People often use the word *one* to avoid over-using *I* in their writing. Although in Britain this is common, in Canada and the United States frequent use of *one* may seem too formal and even a bit pompous:

If <u>one</u> were to apply for the grant, <u>one</u> would find oneself engulfed in so many bureaucratic forms that <u>one's</u> patience would be stretched thin.

As a way out, it's becoming increasingly common in North America to use the third person *his* or *her* as the adjectival form of *one*:

<u>One</u> would find <u>his</u> patience stretched thin.

In any case, try to use *one* sparingly, and don't be afraid of the occasional *I*. The one serious error to avoid is mixing the third person *one* with the second person *you*:

X When <u>one</u> visits the Rockies, <u>you</u> are impressed by the grandeur of the scenery.

In formal academic writing generally, *you* is not an appropriate substitute for *one*.

Using "me" and other objective pronouns

Remembering that it's wrong to say "Jane and me were invited to the party," rather than "Jane and I were invited," many people use the subjective form of the pronoun even when it should be objective:

X   He invited Jane and <u>I</u> to the party.

✓   He invited Jane and <u>me</u> to the party.

The verb *invited* requires an object; *me* is the objective case. The same problem often arises following a preposition:

X   <u>Between</u> you and <u>I</u>, Brown is a bore.

✓   <u>Between</u> you and <u>me</u>, Brown is a bore.

X   Eating well is a problem <u>for we</u> students.

✓   Eating well is a problem <u>for us</u> students.

There are times, however, when the correct case can sound stiff or awkward:

orig.   To whom was the award given?

Rather than keeping to a correct but awkward form, try to reword the sentence:

rev.   Who received the award?

Exceptions for pronouns following prepositions

The rule that a pronoun following a preposition takes the objective case has exceptions. When the preposition is followed by a clause, the pronoun should take the case required by its position in the clause:

X   The Chairman showed some concern over <u>whom would be selected</u> as Dean.

Although the pronoun follows the preposition *over*, it is also the subject of the verb *would be selected* and therefore requires the subjective case:

✓   The Chairman showed some concern over <u>who would be selected</u> as Dean.

Similarly, when a gerund (a word that acts partly as a noun and partly as a verb) is the subject of a clause, the pronoun that modifies it takes the possessive case:

X   Mother was elated by <u>him marrying</u> the Mayor's daughter.

✓   Mother was elated by <u>his marrying</u> the Mayor's daughter.

Troubles with modifying

Adjectives modify nouns; adverbs modify verbs, adjectives, and other adverbs. Do not use an adjective to modify a verb:

X   He played <u>good</u>. (Adjective with verb)
✓   He played <u>well</u>. (Adverb modifying verb)
✓   He played <u>really well</u>. (Adverb modifying adverb)
✓   He had a <u>good style</u>. (Adjective modifying noun)
✓   He had a <u>really good</u> style. (Adverb modifying adjective)

Squinting modifiers

Remember that clarity largely depends on word order: to avoid confusion, the relations between the different parts of a sentence must be clear. Modifiers should therefore be as close as possible to the words they modify. A *squinting modifier* is one that, because of its position, seems to look in two directions at once:

X   She expected <u>in the spring</u> a decline in the stock market.

Was *spring* the time of expectation or the time of the market decline? The logical relation is usually clearest when you place the modifier immediately in front of the element it modifies:

✓   <u>In the spring</u> she <u>expected</u> a decline in the stock market.

✓   She expected a <u>spring decline</u> in the stock market.

Other squinting modifiers can be corrected in the same way:

X   Our English professor gave a lecture on <u>Beowulf</u>, <u>which was well illustrated</u>.

✓   Our English professor gave a <u>well-illustrated lecture</u> on Beowulf.

Dangling modifiers

Modifiers that have no grammatical connection with anything else in the sentence are said to be *dangling*:

X   <u>Walking</u> around the campus in June, the river and trees made a picturesque scene.

Who is doing the walking? Here's another example:

<u>Reflecting</u> on the results of the referendum, it was decided not to press for independence for a while.

Who is doing the reflecting? Clarify the meaning by connecting the dangling modifier to a new subject:

✓ Walking around the campus in June, she thought the river and trees made a picturesque scene.

✓ Reflecting on the results of the referendum, they decided not to press for independence for a while.

Troubles with pairs (and more)

Comparisons

Make sure that your comparisons are complete. The second element in a comparison should be equivalent to the first, whether the equivalence is stated or merely implied:

✗ Today's students have a greater understanding of calculus than their parents.

This sentence suggests that the two things being compared are *calculus* and *parents*. Adding a second verb (*have*) equivalent to the first one shows that the two things being compared are *parents' understanding* and *students' understanding*:

✓ Today's students have a greater understanding of calculus than their parents have.

A similar problem arises in the following comparison:

✗ That cabinet minister is a tiresome man and so are his press conferences.

Press conferences may be tiresome, but they are not *a tiresome man*; to make sense, the two parts of the comparison must be parallel:

✓ That cabinet minister is tiresome, and so are his press conferences.

Correlatives (coordinate constructions)

Constructions such as *both . . . and, not only . . . but,* and *neither . . . nor* are especially tricky. The coordinating term must not come too early, or else one of the parts that come after will not connect with the common element. For the implied comparison to work, the two parts that come after the coordinating term must be grammatically equivalent:

X   He <u>not only</u> bakes cakes <u>but</u> bread.

✓   He bakes <u>not only</u> cakes <u>but</u> bread.

Parallel phrasing

A series of items in a sentence should be phrased in parallel wording. Make sure that all the parts of a parallel construction are in fact equal:

X   Mackenzie King loved <u>his</u> job, <u>his</u> dogs, and mother.

✓   Mackenzie King loved <u>his</u> job, <u>his</u> dogs, and <u>his</u> mother.

Once you have decided to include the pronoun *his* in the first two elements, the third must have it too.

For clarity as well as stylistic grace, keep similar ideas in similar form:

X   He <u>failed</u> Economics and <u>barely passed</u> Statistics, but Political Science <u>was</u> a subject he did well in.

✓   He <u>failed</u> Economics and <u>barely passed</u> Statistics, but <u>did well</u> in Political Science.

9
PUNCTUATION

Punctuation causes students so many problems that it deserves a chapter of its own. If your punctuation is faulty, your readers will be confused and may have to backtrack; worse still, they may be tempted to skip over the rough spots. Punctuation marks are the traffic signals of writing; use them with precision to keep readers moving smoothly through your work.

PERIOD [.]

1. Use a period at the end of a sentence. A period indicates a full stop, not just a pause.

2. Use a period with abbreviations. British style omits the period in certain cases, but North American style usually requires it for abbreviated titles (Mrs., Dr., etc.) as well as place-names (B.C., N.W.T., etc.). Although the abbreviations and acronyms for some organizations include periods, the most common ones generally do not (CARE, CIDA, etc.).

3. Use a period at the end of an indirect question. Do *not* use a question mark:

    ✗   He asked if I wanted a substitute?

    ✓   He asked if I wanted a substitute.

COMMA [,]

Commas are the trickiest of all punctuation marks: even the experts differ on when to use them. Most agree, however, that too many commas are as bad as too few, since they make writing choppy and awkward to read. Certainly recent writers use fewer commas than earlier stylists did. Whenever you are in doubt, let clarity be your guide. The most widely accepted conventions are these:

1. Use a comma to separate two independent clauses joined by a coordinating conjunction (and, but, for, or, nor, yet, so). By signalling that there are two clauses, the comma will prevent the reader from confusing the beginning of the second clause with the end of the first:

> X He went out for dinner with his sister and his room-mate joined them later.

> ✓ He went out for dinner with his sister, and his room-mate joined them later.

When the second clause has the same subject as the first, you have the option of omitting both the second subject and the comma:

> ✓ He can stick-handle well, but he can't shoot.

> ✓ He can stick-handle well but can't shoot.

If you mistakenly punctuate two sentences as if they were one, the result will be a *run-on sentence*; if you use a comma but forget the coordinating conjunction, the result will be a *comma splice*:

> X He took his family to the zoo, it was closed for repairs.

> ✓ He took his family to the zoo, but it was closed for repairs.

Remember that words such as *however, therefore*, and *thus* are *conjunctive adverbs*, not conjunctions: if you use one of them the way you would use a conjunction, the result will again be a *comma splice*:

> X She was accepted into medical school, however, she took a year off to earn her tuition.

> ✓ She was accepted into medical school; however, she took a year off to earn her tuition.

Conjunctive adverbs are often confused with conjunctions. You can distinguish between the two if you remember that a conjunctive adverb's position in a sentence can be changed:

> She was accepted into medical school; she took a year off, <u>however</u>, to earn her tuition.

The position of a conjunction, on the other hand, is invariable; it must be placed between the two clauses:

> She was accepted into medical school, <u>but</u> she took a year off to earn her tuition.

When, in rare cases, the independent clauses are short and closely related, they may be joined by a comma alone:

✓ I came, I saw, I conquered.

A *fused sentence* is a run-on sentence in which independent clauses are slapped together with no punctuation at all:

✗ He watched the hockey game all afternoon the only exercise he got was going to the kitchen between periods.

A fused sentence sounds like breathless babbling—and it's a serious error.

2. Use a comma between items in a series. (Place a coordinating conjunction before the last item):

> She finally found an apartment that was large, bright, and clean.

> Then she had to scrounge around for dishes, pots, cutlery, and a kettle.

The comma before the conjunction is optional:

> She kept a cat, a dog and a budgie.

Sometimes, however, the final comma can help to prevent confusion:

> When we set off on our trip, we were warned about passport thieves, attacks on single women, and baggage loss.

In this case, the comma prevents the reader from thinking that *attacks* are made on *baggage* as well as *single women*.

3. Use a comma to separate adjectives preceding a noun when they modify the same element:

> It was a rainy, windy night.

When the adjectives *do not* modify the same element, however, you should not use a comma:

> It was a pleasant winter outing.

Here *winter* modifies *outing*, but *pleasant* modifies the total phrase *winter outing*. A good way of checking whether or not you need a comma is to see if you can reverse the order of the adjectives. If you can reverse it (*rainy, windy night* or *windy, rainy night*), use a comma; if you can't (*winter pleasant outing*), omit the comma.

4. Use commas to set off an interruption (an interrupting word or phrase is technically called a parenthetical element):

✓ The film, I hear, isn't nearly as good as the book.

✓ My tutor, however, couldn't answer the question.

Remember to put commas on *both sides* of the interruption:

✗ The music, they say was adapted from a piece of Mozart.

✓ The music, they say, was adapted from a piece of Mozart.

5. Use commas to set off words or phrases that provide additional but non-essential information:

Our president, Sue Stephens, does her job well.

The black retriever, his closest companion, went with him everywhere.

Sue Stephens and *his closest companion* are *appositives*: they give additional information about the nouns they refer to (*president* and *retriever*), but the sentences would be understandable without them. Here's another example:

My oldest friend, who lives in Halifax, was married last week.

The phrase *who lives in Halifax* is called a *non-restrictive* modifier, because it does not limit the meaning of the word it modifies (*friend*). Without that modifying clause the sentence would still specify who was married. Since the information the clause provides is not necessary to the meaning of the sentence, you must use commas on both sides to set it off.

In contrast, a *restrictive* modifier is one that provides essential information; therefore it must not be set apart from the element it modifies, and commas should not be used:

The man who came to dinner was my uncle.

Without the clause *who came to dinner*, the reader would not know which man was the uncle.

To avoid confusion, be sure to distinguish carefully between essential and additional information. The difference can be important:

Students, who are not willing to work, should not receive grants.

Students who are not willing to work should not receive grants.

6. Use a comma after an introductory phrase when omitting it would cause confusion:

X   On the balcony above the singers entertained the diners.

✓   On the balcony above, the singers entertained the diners.

X   When he turned away the prisoner disappeared.

✓   When he turned away, the prisoner disappeared.

7. Use a comma to separate elements in dates, addresses, and years:

> February 2, 1983. (Commas are often omitted if the day comes first: 2 February 1983)
>
> 117 Hudson Drive, Edmonton, Alberta.
>
> They lived in Dartmouth, Nova Scotia.

8. Use a comma before a quotation in a sentence:

> He said, ''Life is too short to worry.''
>
> ''The children's safety,'' he warned, ''is in your hands.''

For more formality, you may use a colon (see p. 87).

9. Use a comma with a name followed by a title:

> D. Gunn, Ph.D.
>
> Alice Smith, M.D.

SEMICOLON [;]

1. Use a semicolon to join independent clauses (complete sentences) that are closely related:

> For five days he worked non-stop; by Saturday he was exhausted.
>
> His lecture was confusing; no one could understand the terminology.

A semicolon is especially useful when the second independent clause begins with a conjunctive adverb such as *however, moreover, consequently, nevertheless, in addition,* or *therefore* (usually followed by a comma):

> He bought a bag of doughnuts; however, none of the group was hungry.

Some grammarians may disagree, but it's usually acceptable to follow a semicolon with a coordinating conjunction if the second clause is complicated by other commas:

> John, my cousin, is a keen jogger in all weather; but sometimes, especially in winter, I think it does him more harm than good.

2. Use a semicolon to mark the divisions in a complicated series when individual items themselves need commas. Using a comma to mark the subdivisions and a semicolon to mark the main divisions will help to prevent mix-ups:

> X He invited Prof. Brooks, the vice-principal, Jane Hunter, and John Taylor.

Is the vice-principal a separate person?

> ✓ He invited Prof. Brooks, the vice-principal; Jane Hunter; and John Taylor.

In a case such as this, the elements separated by the semicolon need not be independent clauses.

COLON [:]

A colon indicates that something is to follow.

1. Use a colon before a formal statement or series:

> The winners are the following: Jane, George, and Hugh.

Do not use a colon if the words preceding it do not form a complete sentence:

> X   The winners are: Jane, George and Hugh.

> ✓   The winners are Jane, George, and Hugh.

2. Use a colon for formality before a direct quotation:

> The leaders of the anti-nuclear group repeated their message: "The world needs bread before bombs."

DASH [--]

A dash creates an abrupt pause, emphasizing the words that follow. (Never use dashes as casual substitutes for other punctuation: overuse can detract from the calm, well-reasoned effect you want.)

1. Use a dash to stress a word or phrase:

The British--as a matter of honour--vowed to retake the islands.

Foster was well received in the legislature--at first.

2. Use a dash in interrupted or unfinished dialogue:

"It's a matter--to put it delicately--of personal hygiene."

In typing, use two hyphens together, with no spaces on either side, to show a dash.

EXCLAMATION MARK [!]

An exclamation mark helps to show emotion or feeling. It is usually found in dialogue:

"Woe is me!" she mourned.

In academic writing, you should use it only in those rare cases when you want to give a point an emotional emphasis:

He concluded that inflation would decrease in 1981. Some forecast!

QUOTATION MARKS [" " or ' ']

Quotation marks are usually double in American style and single in British. In Canada either is accepted—just be consistent.

1. Use quotation marks to signify direct discourse (the actual words of a speaker):

I asked, "What is the matter?"

He said, "I have a pain in my big toe."

2. Use quotation marks to show that words themselves are the issue:

The term "love" in tennis comes from the French word for "egg."

Alternatively, you may italicize or underline the terms in question.

Sometimes quotation marks are used to mark a slang word or an inappropriate usage, to show that the writer is aware of the difficulty:

Hitler's "final solution" was the most barbaric act of this century.

Use this device only when necessary; usually it's better to let the context show your attitude, or to choose another term.

3. Use quotation marks to enclose the titles of poems, short stories, paintings, songs, films, and articles in books or journals. In contrast, titles of books, paintings, or music are italicized or underlined:

> The story I like best in Robert Weaver's <u>Canadian Short Stories</u> is "Bernadette" by Mavis Gallant.

4. Use quotation marks to enclose quotations within quotations (single or double depending on your primary style):

> He said, "Hitler's 'final solution' was the most barbaric act of this century."

PLACEMENT OF PUNCTUATION WITH QUOTATION MARKS

Both the British and the American practices are accepted in Canada. British style usually places the punctuation outside the quotation marks, unless it is actually part of the quotation. The American practice, followed in this book, is increasingly common in Canada:

- A comma or period always goes inside the quotation marks:

  > He said, "Give me another chance," but I replied, "You've had enough chances."

- A semicolon or colon always goes outside the quotation marks:

  > George wants to watch "Second City"; I'd rather watch the hockey game.

- A question mark, dash, or exclamation mark goes inside quotation marks if it is part of the quotation, but outside if it is not:

  > He asked, "What is for dinner?"
  >
  > Did he really call the boss a "lily-livered hypocrite"?
  >
  > His speech was hardly an appeal for "blood, sweat and tears"!
  >
  > I was just whispering to Mary, "That instructor is a--" when suddenly he glanced at me.

- When a reference is given parenthetically (in round brackets) at the end of a quotation, the quotation marks precede the parentheses and the sentence punctuation follows them:

  > Lipsey suggests that we should "abandon the Foreign Investment Review Agency" (<u>Globe and Mail</u>, 12 April 1983).

APOSTROPHE [']

The apostrophe forms the possessive case for nouns and some pronouns.

1. **Add an apostrophe followed by "s" to**
   - all singular and plural nouns *not* ending in *s*: *cat's*, *women's*.
   - singular *proper* nouns ending in *s*: *Keats's*, *Sis's* (but note that the final *s* can be omitted if the word has a number of them already and would sound awkward, as in *Jesus'* or certain classical names).
   - indefinite pronouns: *someone's*, *anybody's*, etc;

2. **Add an apostrophe to plural nouns ending in "s":** *families'*, *houses'*, *cars'*.

PARENTHESES [( )]

1. **Use parentheses to enclose an explanation, example, or qualification.** Parentheses show that the enclosed material is of incidental importance to the main idea. They make a less pronounced interruption than a dash, but a more pronounced one than a comma:

> My wife (the eldest of five children) is a superb cook and carpenter.

> His latest plan (according to neighbours) is to dam the creek.

Remember that although punctuation should not precede parentheses, it may follow them if required by the sense of the sentence:

> I like coffee in the morning (if it's not instant), but she prefers tea.

If the parenthetical statement comes between two complete sentences, it should be punctuated as a sentence, with the period inside the parentheses:

> I finished my last essay on April 30. (It was on Aristotle's ethics.) Fortunately, I had three weeks free to study for the exam.

2. **Use parentheses to enclose references.** See Chapters 10 and 11 for details.

BRACKETS [ ]

Brackets are square enclosures, not to be confused with parentheses (which are round).

1. Use brackets to set off a remark of your own within a quotation. They show that the words enclosed are not those of the person quoted:

> Fox maintains, "Obstacles to western unification [in the eighties] are as many as they are serious."

Brackets are sometimes used to enclose *sic* (Latin for *thus*), which is used after an error, such as a misspelling, to show that the mistake was in the original. *Sic* should be underlined:

> The politician, in his letter to constitutents, wrote about "these parlouse [sic] times of economic difficulty."

HYPHEN [-]

1. Use a hyphen if you must divide a word at the end of a line. When a word is too long to fit at the end of a line, it's best to keep it in one piece by starting a new line. If you must divide, however, remember these rules:

- Divide between syllables.
- Never divide a one-syllable word.
- Never leave one letter by itself.
- Divide double consonants except when they come before a suffix, in which case divide before the suffix:

> ar-rangement
> embar-rassment
> fall-ing
> pass-able

When the second consonant has been added to form the suffix, keep it with the suffix:

> refer-ral
> begin-ning

2. Use a hyphen to separate the parts of certain compound words:

> sister-in-law, vice-consul (compound nouns)
>
> test-drive, proof-read (compound verbs)
>
> well-considered plan, twentieth-century attitudes
> (compound adjectives used as modifiers preceding nouns)

When you are *not* using such expressions adjectivally, do *not* hyphenate them:

> The plan was <u>well considered</u>.
> These are attitudes of the <u>twentieth century</u>.

After long-time use, some compound nouns drop the hyphen. When in doubt, check a dictionary.

3. Use a hyphen with certain prefixes (*all-*, *self-*, *ex-*, and those prefixes preceding a proper name):

> all-party, self-imposed, ex-jockey, anti-nuclear, pro-Canadian.

4. Use a hyphen to emphasize contrasting prefixes:

> The coach agreed to give both <u>pre-</u> and <u>post-game</u> interviews.

5. Use a hyphen to separate written-out compound numbers from one to a hundred and compound fractions used as modifiers:

> eighty-one years ago
> seven-tenths full

6. Use a hyphen to separate parts of inclusive numbers or dates:

> the years 1890-1914
> pages 3-40

ELLIPSIS [. . .]

1. Use an ellipsis to show an omission from a quotation:

> He reported that "the drought in the thirties, to many farming families in the west . . . resembled a biblical plague, even to the locusts."

If the omission comes at the end of a sentence, the ellipsis is followed by a fourth period.

2. Use an ellipsis to show that a series of numbers continues indefinitely:

> 1, 3, 5, 7, 9 ...

10
DOCUMENTATION
in the humanities

This chapter is specifically intended as a guide for handling quotations, footnotes, and bibliographies in humanities subjects; however, it may also be useful for some subjects in the social sciences.

QUOTATIONS

Quotations can add authority to your writing as well as help you avoid charges of plagiarism. But you should use them with care: never quote a passage just because it sounds impressive. Be sure that it really adds to your discussion, either by expressing an idea with special force or cogency, or by giving substance to a debatable point.

Guidelines for incorporating quotations

1. Integrate the quotation so that it makes sense in the context of your discussion and fits in grammatically:

   ✗ Henry Ford had little knowledge of history. "History is bunk," but his opinion is not one that many educated people would accept.

   ✓ Henry Ford had little knowledge of history. His opinion that "history is bunk" is not one that many educated people would accept.

2. Be accurate. Reproduce the exact wording, punctuation, and spelling of the original, including any errors. You can acknowledge a mistake by inserting the Latin word *sic* in brackets after it (see p. 91). If you want to underline part of the quotation for emphasis, add *my emphasis* in brackets at the end.

3. Include as part of your text, enclosed in quotation marks,
   - not more than four lines of prose;
   - not more than three lines of verse. Use a slash (/) to indicate the end of a line:

   > When Keats says, "That I may drink, and leave the world unseen/And with thee fade away into the forest dim," he is referring to the temptations of death.

4. Set off from your text by indenting (five to ten spaces) and omitting quotation marks
   - five or more lines of prose;
   - four or more lines of verse.

   A long quotation is usually single-spaced and introduced by a colon. If the first line of your quotation is the first sentence of a new paragraph, indent the first line an extra three spaces:

   > Machiavelli recognized the ability of a republic to change with the times:
   >> Therefore, the truth is that a republic is of longer duration and has a much better fortune than a principality, for a republic, by virtue of its diverse citizenry, can better accommodate itself to the changeability of conditions than can a prince.

5. For a quotation within a quotation, use single quotation marks:

   > A news report described the scene this way: "When the crowd heard de Gaulle shout, 'Vive le Québec libre!', they roared with approval."

6. If you want to omit something from the original, use ellipsis marks (three single-spaced periods):

   > "The uprising was the result of indifference on the part of national leaders . . . and mismanagement on the part of civil servants."

If the omission is at the end of a sentence, add a fourth period.

To omit a full line of a poem, use a full line of single-spaced periods:

> Cedar and jagged fir
> . . . .
> against the gray
> and cloud-piled sky

7. If you want to insert an explanatory comment of your own into a quotation, enclose it in square brackets:

> "At private meetings, three western premiers [Bennett, Lougheed, and Devine] strenuously objected to the federal proposal."

Note that brackets are square, not round; if your typewriter doesn't have a key for brackets, mark them by hand.

FOOTNOTES

Footnotes are required in most academic writing to allow the reader to check sources and verify information. If you are quoting or summarizing other people's ideas, you also need them to avoid charges of plagiarism. Too many notes can be distracting, however, since they interrupt the reader's progress. To avoid clutter, remember that you don't need references to common knowledge or undisputed facts. As well, try to include in the text as much as possible of the footnote information, keeping the note itself as brief as possible.

Use footnotes in four specific instances:

- to identify quotations;
- to acknowledge and give exact references to the words and ideas of others—even if you paraphrase or summarize them in your own words, rather than quote directly;
- to provide additional relevant information or comments that are difficult to fit into the text;
- to refer to other parts of a long discussion.

Format for references to outside sources

1. For the reader's convenience, you may place your footnote at the bottom of the page on which the citation appears. Be sure to leave enough space; don't cram it into the margin at the bottom of the page. You should also leave a quadruple space between the text and the footnote, to make the division clear.
2. If you choose to place all your footnotes at the end of your writing you may call them *endnotes*. Using a separate page, underline your title—*Footnotes* or *Endnotes*—and centre the notes under it. Leave a triple space between the title and the first entry.
3. Whichever format you choose, remember to number your notes consecutively, using arabic numerals, and to put the corresponding

number at the end of the sentence in which you make each reference, using superscript (a number slightly raised above the line of words). The numbers should follow all end punctuation.

4. Bottom-of-the-page footnotes should be indented the same number of spaces that you use for a new paragraph. In student writing, they should be single-spaced, in contrast to the double-spaced text. Leave a double space between entries.

The following examples of documentation are restricted to the most common kinds of footnote and bibliographic references. For a more comprehensive survey, consult one of the following:

- *MLA Handbook for Writers of Research Papers, Theses, and Dissertations* (New York: Modern Language Association, 1977).
- Kate Turabian, *A Manual for Writers of Term Papers, Theses, and Dissertations,* 3rd ed., rev. (Chicago: Univ. of Chicago Press, 1967).
- Roy Wiles, *Scholarly Reporting in the Humanities*, 4th ed., rev. (Toronto: Univ. of Toronto Press, 1972).

Footnotes for first references

Book by one author:

[1]Desmond Morton, Ministers and Generals: Politics and the Canadian Militia (Toronto: Univ. of Toronto Press, 1970), 20.

Capitalize the first letter in the title and subtitle, as well as the first letters of all words except for articles, prepositions, and conjunctions. If you give full bibliographic references later, you may omit subtitles in notes. Familiar terms such as *University* or *editor* may be abbreviated.

Book by two authors:

[2]Clara Thomas and John Lennox, William Arthur Deacon: A Canadian Literary Life (Toronto: Univ. of Toronto Press, 1982), 32.

Although the title page may list more than one place of publication (say, Toronto and Buffalo), you need only name the first place in your reference.

Book by three or more authors:

[3]Richard G. Lipsey et al., Economics, 4th ed. (New York: Harper and Row, 1982), 67.

Edition other than the first:

> ⁴Paul W. Fox, ed., Politics: Canada, 4th ed. (Toronto: McGraw-Hill Ryerson, 1977), 3.

Book with one editor:

> ⁵Germaine Warkentin, ed., Stories from Ontario: A Selection (Toronto: Macmillan, 1974).

When the publisher's full title is lengthy, you may use its familiar short form; thus *Macmillan of Canada Ltd.* becomes simply *Macmillan.*

Book with two editors:

> ⁶Ralph Kruyeger and R. Charles Bryfogle, eds., Urban Problems (Toronto: Holt, 1971).

Books by one author edited by another:

> ⁷Hugh MacLennan, The Other Side of Hugh MacLennan, Elspeth Cameron, ed. (Toronto: Macmillan, 1978).

Books by one author translated by another:

> ⁸Plato's Republic, G.M.A. Grube, trans. (Indianapolis: Huckett, 1974).

You need not list the author's name when it is part of the title.

Book in more than one volume:

> ⁹Donald Creighton, John A. Macdonald (Toronto: Macmillan, 1955-56), 2 vols.

Article by one author in a work edited by another:

> ¹⁰Michael Hornyansky, ''Is Your English Destroying Your Image?'' in In the Name of Language, Joseph Gold, ed. (Toronto: Macmillan, 1975).

Article in a journal with separate issues:

> ¹¹Jeffrey M. Heath, ''The Private Language of Evelyn Waugh,'' English Studies in Canada 2, no. 3 (Fall 1976), 329-39.

The abbreviations *p.* or *pp.* may be used to indicate page numbers, but increasingly they are omitted from references. Most page numbers may be contracted to avoid unnecessary repetition (for example, *33-7, 465-82, 1277-9*); however, numbers between *10* and *20* should always be written in full (*10-11, 12-15, 214-18, 1342-1480*). If the issue of the journal in which the article appears is one of several bound together to form a single volume with continuous page numbers, you may leave out the week or month of publication. Just give the volume number, year (in parentheses), and page numbers:

> [1]George Woodcock, "Anarchist Phases and Personalities," Queen's Quarterly 87 (1980), 82-97.

Unsigned article in an encyclopedia:

> [12]Encyclopaedia Britannica: Micropaedia, 1974 ed., s.v. "Riel, Louis".

When citing entries in dictionaries and other unsigned, alphabetically arranged reference books, it's best to use *s.v.* (*sub verbo*, "under the word") rather than the volume and page numbers.

When an entry is signed, list the author's name first.

Government document:

> [13]Canada Dept. of Labour, Women's Bureau, Changing Patterns in Women's Employment (Ottawa: Queen's Printer, 1966), 70.

Proceedings:

> [14]Canadian Institute of International Affairs, Proceedings of Lester B. Pearson Conference on Canada-United States Relationship (Niagara-on-the-Lake, Ont.: n.p., 1976), 32.

The abbreviation *n.p.* indicates that there is no publisher.

Book review:

> [15]Grant Reuber, rev. of On Economics and Society by Harry G. Johnson, Queen's Quarterly 83, no. 1 (Spring 1976), 129-30.

Signed newspaper article:

> [16]Robert Gibbens, "Quebec Government Reviews Equipment Purchasing Policy," Globe and Mail, Report on Business, 2 Dec. 1982, B3.

Unsigned newspaper article:

> [17]"Financing System Called Damaging to National Growth,"
> Globe and Mail, 14 July 1982, 4.

Footnotes for subsequent references

1. Subsequent footnote references should usually be brief, including only the author's name and the page number:

   Morton, 22.

2. Instead of putting subsequent references as footnotes, you may enclose them in parentheses and include them in the body of the text, before the final punctuation in the referring sentence:

   > Educators can also be trendy; the charge may be fair that those who deplore a return to the basics are "suffering from delirium trendens" (Hornyansky, 93).

3. If you are citing more than one work by an author, add the title (it may be in shortened form) after the author's name:

   (Frye: Modern Century, 42)

4. If you are repeatedly referring to a single primary source, in references after the first you may simply enclose the page numbers in parentheses. If you are discussing a drama, refer to the act, scene, and line; if discussing a poem, refer to the verse and/or line.

BIBLIOGRAPHIES

A bibliography is an alphabetical list of both those works cited in an essay and those found useful in preparing it. Your instructor may not require a bibliography if you document your references fully in footnotes, but it's a good idea to provide one.

Format

The format for bibliographies differs slightly from that for footnotes:
1. Use a separate page at the end of your essay, with an underlined heading, *Bibliography*, centred on the page.
2. Single-space all entries, leaving a double space between entries and a triple space between the heading and the first entry. Do not indent entries.
3. Do not number entries, but *list them alphabetically* by the author's

or editor's surname. If no author is given, begin with the first significant word in the title.

4. Begin each bibliographic entry at the margin and indent any subsequent line five spaces.

5. Separate the main divisions by periods (rather than the commas and parentheses used in footnotes).

Book:

> Fox, Paul W., ed. Politics: Canada. 4th ed. Toronto: McGraw-Hill Ryerson, 1977.
>
> Frye, Northrop. Anatomy of Criticism: Four Essays. Princeton: Princeton Univ. Press, 1957.

If you include more than one work by a particular author, place the entries in alphabetical order by title (not counting the initial articles). Give the name in the first entry only. For subsequent entries, type ten hyphens and a period. Leave two spaces and give the next title:

> Hood, Hugh. The Governor's Bridge Is Closed. Toronto: Oberon, 1973.
>
> ----------. A New Athens. Toronto: Oberon, 1977.

If there is more than one author or editor, use inverted order for the first name only and natural order for the rest:

> Thomas, Clara and John Lennox: William Arthur Deacon: A Canadian Literary Life. Toronto: Univ. of Toronto Press, 1982.

Article in a book:

> Ward, Barbara. "The First International Nation." In Canada: A Guide to the Peaceable Kingdom, 45-9. William Kilbourn, ed. Toronto: Macmillan, 1970.

Article in a journal:

> Heath, Jeffrey M. "The Private Language of Evelyn Waugh." English Studies in Canada 2, no. 3 (Fall 1976), 329-39.

11
DOCUMENTATION
in the sciences

Methods of documentation in the sciences may differ widely even within a single discipline: always check with your instructor or department to make sure you are following the preferred practice. If your subject is one of the social sciences not listed in this chapter, find out whether your department uses the system for the humanities.

Documentation in a scientific report or essay differs from that in a humanities paper in two important ways:

1. Instead of footnotes, it uses brief references (termed *citations*) in the text itself.

2. Instead of a bibliography, it uses a section entitled *References* or *Literature Cited*, which lists only those works *directly referred to* in the text; other works consulted are not listed. The rules regarding plagiarism are the same, however: see pp. 12 and 95.

This chapter outlines the two basic methods (alphabetical and consecutive)[1] for listing documentation, and the conventions usually followed in each discipline. It also recommends journals that you may use as models; when the models for a particular subject differ, choose one method and follow it consistently.

ALPHABETICAL LISTING

In the text

1. The citation should usually be placed at the end of the sentence in which you refer to the work, with the author's surname and the year of publication in parentheses:

   > Biologists have recently analysed the vascular flora in the boreal forests south of James Bay (Carleton and Maycock, 1980).

2. When referring to a specific page or table, include the number:

> (Carleton and Maycock, 1980, p. 121).
> (Smith, 1982, Table 3).

3. If you have already given the author's name in the text itself, all you need to add is the year:

> The work of Thaler and Plowright (1980) supports this hypothesis.

4. When citing two authors, give both names; when citing more than two, give the name of the first only, followed by *et al.*:

> O'Day et al. investigated this autoinhibitor of zygote giant cell formation (1981).

In the reference section

Although specific details vary depending on the subject (see the sample entries below), all subjects in the alphabetical group share some features of reference style in common. Here are the general guidelines:

1. List your references alphabetically by author, surname first followed by initials; do not number them.
2. For a work with two or more authors, list all their names (in most cases, only the first author's name should be reversed; give the rest in natural order).
3. When citing more than one work by a particular author, list the entries in chronological order (the date should usually follow the author's name); for works published in the same year, add a letter marker to each date (1982a, 1982b, etc.). After the first entry, omit the author's name (type ten hyphens and a period, then leave two spaces and continue: see p. 100).
4. For references to journals, always include the volume, issue, and page numbers.

Sample entries

In addition to the basic guidelines listed above, be sure to note the special features of your subject's style. For more details, see the journals suggested as models.

Anthropology. Book titles are capitalized (for the rules, see p. 96) but not underlined. The place of publication precedes the publisher's name. Model: *Canadian Journal of Anthropology* or *American Anthropologist*.

Book:

McHugh, T. 1972. The Time of the Buffalo. New York: Knopf.

Journal:

Mohr, A. 1980. Wishram birth and obstetrics. Ethnology 19:42 7-445.

Astronomy. Book titles are capitalized (for the rules, see p. 96) and underlined. The date is placed in parentheses, as are the publisher's name and the place of publication. The titles of articles are omitted and those of journals abbreviated. Volume numbers are underlined. Model: *The Astronomical Journal*.

Book:

Baade, W. (1963). The Evolution of Stars and Galaxies (Harvard Univ., Cambridge, Mass.).

Journal:

Smith, R.M., G.V. Bicknell, A.R. Hyland, and T.J. Jones (1983). Astrophys. J. 266, 69-72.

Biology. Book titles are capitalized (see p. 96) but not underlined. The publisher's name precedes the place of publication. Journal titles may be abbreviated; for the accepted forms, see the *1976 Biosis List of Serials*. Model: *Canadian Journal of Botany* or *Canadian Journal of Zoology*.

Book:

Radford, A.E., W. C. Dickinson, J.R. Massey, and C.R. Bell. 1974. Vascular Plant Systematics. Harper and Row, New York.

Journal:

Ouchterlony, O. 1958. Diffusion-in-gel methods for immunological analysis. Prog. Allergy, 5: 1-78.

Earth Sciences. Titles are not underlined. The publisher's name precedes the place of publication. Model: *Canadian Journal of Earth Sciences* or *Geographical Society of America Bulletin*.

Book:

> Chow, V.T. 1969. Handbook of applied hydrology. McGraw-
> Hill, New York.

Journal:

> Dell, C. 1963. A study of the mineralogical composition of
> sand in northern Ontario. Canadian Journal of Soil Science,
> 43, pp. 189-200.

Psychology. The titles of books and journals are underlined, as are
the volume numbers of journals. All authors' names are reversed (surname before initials), even when there is more than one. The date of
publication follows the title of the book or journal. For more details,
see the *Publication Manual* of the American Psychological Association
(2nd ed.).

Book:

> Craik, F.I.M., and Trehuk, S.E. Aging and cognition pro-
> cesses. New York: Plenum Press. 1983.

Journal:

> Moscovitch, M. Right-hemisphere language. Topics in Lan-
> guage Disorders, 1981, 1, 4.

CONSECUTIVE LISTING

In the text

Instead of giving publication details in the text itself, use consecutive
numbers (slightly raised above the line) to direct the reader to the
reference section at the end of the paper:

> These findings are supported by Becker and Poë.[3]

Use the same number for every subsequent reference to the same work.

In the reference section

1. Arrange the references in the same order as in the text and number
   them accordingly.
2. Abbreviate journal titles.

Sample entries

Chemistry. Book titles are usually enclosed in quotation marks; article titles are omitted. The author's name is listed with the surname preceding the initials. For the correct abbreviations of journal titles, see *CASSI—Chemical Abstracts Service Source Index* (Columbus, Ohio: The American Chemical Society, 1980). Model: *Journal of the American Chemical Society*.

Book:

   1. Hoffman, B.E.J. "Coal gasifiers." The Energon Co.: Laramie, Wyoming, 1981; pp15-50.

Journal:

   2. Still, I.W.J.; Kutney, G.W. J. Org Chem. 1981, <u>46</u>, 4911.

Physics. Authors' names are listed in natural order. The titles of articles are omitted. For journal abbreviations, see *CASSI—Chemical Abstracts Service Source Index* (Columbus, Ohio: The American Chemical Society, 1980). Model: *Canadian Journal of Physics*; or see the *Style Manual* of the American Institute of Physics.

Book:

   1. P. Jones and J. Jackson (Editors). Elections in Fluids. Pergamon. London, 1981.

Journal:

   2. D.J. Dunlop and M.B. Zinn. Can. J. Earth Sci., <u>17</u>, 1275-1285 (1980).

NOTE

¹This division is based on that in *Notes on the Preparation of Essays in the Arts and Sciences* (Peterborough, Ont.: The Self-Instruction Centre, Trent University, 1979).

CATCHLIST
of misused words and phrases

accept, except. Accept is a verb meaning to *receive affirmatively*; **except**, when used as a verb, means to *exclude*:

> I <u>accept</u> your offer.
> The teacher <u>excepted</u> him from the general punishment.

accompanied by, accompanied with. Use **accompanied by** for people; **accompanied with** for objects:

> He was <u>accompanied</u> by his wife.
> The brochure arrived, <u>accompanied with</u> a discount coupon.

advice, advise. Advice is a noun, **advise** a verb:

> He was <u>advised</u> to ignore the others' <u>advice</u>.

affect, effect. As a verb to **affect** means to *influence*; as a noun it's a technical psychological term. The verb to **effect** means to *bring about*. The noun means *result*. In most cases, you will be safe if you remember to use **affect** for the verb and **effect** for the noun:

> The eye drops <u>affect</u> his vision.
> The <u>effect</u> of higher government spending is higher inflation.

all together, altogether. All together means *in a group*; **altogether** is an adverb meaning *entirely*:

> He was <u>altogether</u> certain that the children were <u>all together</u>.

alot. Write as two separate words: *a lot*.

allusion, illusion. An **allusion** is an indirect reference to something; an **illusion** is a false perception:

> The rock image is an <u>allusion</u> to the myth of Sisyphus.
> He thought he saw a sea monster, but it was an <u>illusion</u>.

among, between. Use **among** for three or more persons or objects, **between** for two:

> Between you and me, there's trouble among the team members.

amoral, immoral. Amoral means *non-moral* or outside the moral sphere; **immoral** means *wicked*:

> As an art critic, he was amoral in his judgements.
> That immoral performance should be restricted to adults.

amount, number. Use **amount** for money or noncountable quantities; use **number** for countable items:

> No amount of wealth or number of expensive possessions will make up for a lack of love.

anyways. Non-standard English: use *anyway*.

as, because. As is a weaker conjunction than **because** and may be confused with *when*:

> As I was working, I ate at my desk.
> Because I was working, I ate at my desk.

> He arrived as I was leaving.
> He arrived when I was leaving.

as to. A common feature of bureaucratese; replace it with a single-word preposition such as *about* or *on*:

> X They were concerned as to the range of disagreement.
> ✓ They were concerned about the range of disagreement.

> X They recorded his comments as to the treaty.
> ✓ They recorded his comments on the treaty.

bad, badly. Bad is an adjective meaning *not good*:

> The meat tastes bad.
> He felt bad about forgetting the dinner party.

Badly is an adverb meaning *not well;* when used with the verbs **want** or **need**, it means *very much*:

> She thought he played the villain's part badly.
> I badly need a new suit.

beside, besides. Beside is a preposition meaning *next to*:

> She worked beside her assistant.

Besides has two uses: as a preposition it means *in addition to*; as a conjunctive adverb it means *moreover*:

> Besides recommending the changes, the consultants are implementing them.
> Besides, it was hot and we wanted to rest.

between. See **among.**

bring, take. One **brings** something to a closer place and **takes** it to a farther one.

can, may. Can means to *be able*; **may** means to *have permission*:

> Can you fix the lock?
> May I have another piece of cake?

In speech, **can** is used to cover both meanings: in formal writing, however, you should observe the distinction.

can't hardly. A faulty combination of the phrases **can't** and **can hardly**. Use one or the other of them instead:

> He can't swim.
> He can hardly swim.

capital, capitol. As a noun **capital** may refer to a seat of government, the top of a pillar, an upper-case letter, or accumulated wealth. **Capitol** refers only to a specific American—or ancient Roman—legislative building.

complement, compliment. The verb to **complement** means to *complete*; to **compliment** means to *praise*:

> His engineering skill complements the skills of the designers.
> I complimented her on her outstanding report.

continual, continuous. Continual means *repeated over a period of time*; **continuous** means *constant* or *without interruption*:

> The strikes caused continual delays in building the road.
> In August, it rained continuously for five days.

could of. Incorrect, as are **might of**, **should of**, and **would of**. Replace **of** with *have*:

> ✗ He <u>could of</u> done it.
> ✓ He <u>could have</u> done it.
> ✓ They <u>might have</u> been there.
> ✓ I <u>should have</u> known.
> ✓ We <u>would have</u> left earlier.

council, counsel. Council is a noun meaning an *advisory* or *deliberative assembly*. **Counsel** as a noun means *advice* or *lawyer*; as a verb it means to *give advice*:

> The college <u>council</u> meets on Tuesday.
> We respect his <u>counsel</u>, since he's seldom wrong.
> As a camp <u>counsellor</u>, you may need to <u>counsel</u> parents as well as children.

criterion, criteria. A **criterion** is a standard for judging something. **Criteria** is the plural of **criterion** and thus requires a plural verb:

> <u>These</u> are my <u>criteria</u> for selecting the paintings.

data. The plural of *datum*, **data** is increasingly treated as a singular noun, but this usage is not yet acceptable in formal prose: use a plural verb.

different than. Incorrect. Use either **different from** (American usage) or **different to** (British).

disinterested, uninterested. Disinterested implies impartiality or neutrality; **uninterested** implies a lack of interest:

> As a <u>disinterested</u> observer, he was in a good position to judge the issue fairly.
> <u>Uninterested</u> in the proceedings, he yawned repeatedly.

due to. Although increasingly used to mean *because of*, **due** is an adjective and therefore needs to modify something:

> ✗ Due to his impatience, we lost the contract. [<u>Due</u> is dangling]
> ✓ The loss was <u>due to</u> his impatience.

farther, further. Farther refers to distance, **further** to extent:

> He paddled <u>farther</u> than his friends.
> He explained the plan <u>further</u>.

good, well. Good is an adjective, not an adverb. **Well** can be both: as an adverb, it means *effectively*; as an adjective, it means *healthy*:

> The pear sauce tastes <u>good</u>.
> She is a <u>good</u> golfer.
> She plays golf <u>well</u>.
> At last, he is <u>well</u> again after his long bout of flu.

hanged, hung. Hanged means *executed by hanging.* **Hung** means *suspended* or *clung to*:

> He was <u>hanged</u> at dawn for the murder.
> He <u>hung</u> the picture.
> He <u>hung</u> to the boat when it capsized.

hopefully. Use **hopefully** as an adverb meaning *full of hope*:

> She scanned the horizon <u>hopefully</u>, waiting for her friend's ship to appear.

In formal writing, using **hopefully** to mean *I hope* is still frowned upon, although increasingly common; it's better to use *I hope*:

> ✗ <u>Hopefully</u> we'll make a bigger profit this year.
> ✓ <u>I hope</u> we'll make a bigger profit this year.

imply, infer. Imply refers to what a statement suggests; **infer** relates to the audience's interpretation:

> His letter <u>implied</u> that he was lonely.
> I <u>inferred</u> from his letter that he would welcome a visit.

irregardless. Redundant; use *regardless.*

its, it's. Its is a form of possessive pronoun; **it's** is a contraction of *it is.* Many people mistakenly put an apostrophe in **its** in order to show possession:

> ✗ The cub wanted <u>it's</u> mother.
> ✓ The cub wanted <u>its</u> mother.
> ✓ <u>It's</u> time to leave.

less, fewer. Use **less** for money and things that are not countable; use **fewer** for things that are:

> Now that he's earning <u>less</u> money he's going to <u>fewer</u> movies.

lie, lay. To **lie** means to *assume a horizontal position*; to **lay** means to *put down*. The changes of tense often cause confusion:

Present	Past	Past participle
lie	lay	lain
lay	laid	laid

like, as. Like is a preposition, but it is often wrongly used as a conjunction. To join two independent clauses, use the conjunction **as**:

   ✗   I want to progress <u>like</u> you have this year.
   ✓   I want to progress <u>as</u> you have this year.

   ✓   Prof. Dodd is <u>like</u> my old school principal.

might of. See **could of.**

myself, me. Myself is an intensifier of, not a substitute for, *I* or *me*:

   ✗   He gave it to John and <u>myself.</u>
   ✓   He gave it to John and <u>me.</u>

   ✗   Jane and <u>myself</u> are invited.
   ✓   Jane and <u>I</u> are invited.

   ✓   <u>Myself</u>, I would prefer a swivel chair.

nor, or. Use **nor** with **neither** and **or** by itself or with **either**:

     He is <u>neither</u> overworked <u>nor</u> underfed.
     The plant is <u>either</u> diseased <u>or</u> dried out.

off of. Remove the unnecessary **of**:

   ✗   The fence kept the children <u>off of</u> the premises.
   ✓   The fence kept the children <u>off</u> the premises.

phenomenon. A singular noun: the plural is **phenomena.**

principal, principle. As an adjective, **principal** means *main* or *most important*; a **principal** is the head of a school. A **principle** is a *law* or *controlling idea*:

     Our <u>principal</u> aim is to reduce the deficit.
     Our <u>principal</u>, Prof. Smart, retires next year.
     We are defending the island as a matter of <u>principle.</u>

rational, rationale. Rational is an adjective meaning *logical* or *able to reason*. **Rationale** is a noun meaning *explanation*:

     That was not a <u>rational</u> decision.
     The president sent around a memo with a <u>rationale</u> for his proposal.

real, really. The adjective **real** should never be used as an adverb; use *really* instead:

✓ We had <u>real</u> maple syrup with our pancakes.

✗ It was <u>real</u> good.
✓ It was <u>really</u> good.

set, sit. To **sit** means to *rest on the buttocks*; to **set** means to *put* or *place*:

After standing so long, you'll want to <u>sit</u> down.
Please <u>set</u> the bowl on the table.

should of. See **could of**.

their, there. **Their** is the possessive form of the third person plural pronoun. **There** is usually an adverb, meaning *at that place* or *at that point*; sometimes it is used as an expletive (an introductory word in a sentence):

They parked <u>their</u> bikes <u>there</u>.
<u>There</u> is no point in arguing with you.

to, too, two. **To** is a preposition, as well as part of the infinitive form of a verb:

We went <u>to town</u> in order <u>to shop</u>.

Too is an adjective showing degree (the soup is *too* hot) or an adverb meaning *moreover*. **Two** is the spelled version of the number 2.

while. To avoid misreadings, use **while** only when you mean *at the same time that*. Do not use it as a substitute for *although, whereas,* or *but*:

✗ <u>While</u> he's getting fair marks, he'd like to do better.
✗ I headed for home, <u>while</u> she decided to stay.
✓ He fell asleep <u>while</u> he was reading.

-wise. Never use **-wise** as a suffix to form new words when you mean *with regard to*:

✗ <u>Sales-wise</u>, the company did better last year.
✓ <u>With regard to sales,</u> the company did better last year.
(or) The company's sales increased last year.

your, you're. **Your** is a pronominal adjective used to show possession; **you're** is a contraction of *you are*:

<u>You're</u> likely to miss <u>your</u> train.

GLOSSARY

abstract
a summary accompanying a formal scientific report or paper, briefly outlining the contents.

abstract language
theoretical language removed from concrete particulars: e.g., *justice, goodness, truth* (cf. **concrete language**).

acronym
a word made up of the first letters of a group of words: e.g., *NATO* for *North Atlantic Treaty Organization*.

active voice
see **voice**.

adjective
a word that modifies or describes a noun or pronoun, hence a kind of noun marker: e.g., *red, beautiful, solemn*. An **adjectival phrase** or **adjectival clause** is a group of words modifying a noun or pronoun.

adverb
a word that modifies or qualifies a verb, adjective, or adverb, often answering a question such as *how? why? when?* or *where?*: e.g., *slowly, fortunately, early, abroad*. An **adverbial phrase** or **adverbial clause** is a group of words modifying a verb, adjective, or adverb: e.g., *by force, in revenge*. See also **conjunctive adverb**.

agreement
consistency in tense, number, or person between related parts of a sentence: e.g., between subject and verb, or noun and related pronoun.

ambiguity
vague or equivocal language; meaning that can be taken two ways.

antecedent (referent)
the noun for which a pronoun stands.

appositive
a word or phrase that identifies a preceding noun or pronoun: e.g., *Mrs. Jones,* **my aunt,** *is sick*. The second phrase is said to be *in apposition* to the first.

article
a word that precedes a noun and shows whether the noun is definite or indefinite; a kind of determiner or noun-marker. **Indefinite article:** *a (an)*. **Definite article**: *the*.

assertion
a positive statement or claim: e.g., *The Senate is irrelevant*.

auxiliary
a verb used in combination with another verb to create a verb phrase; a helping verb used to create certain tenses and emphases: e.g., *could, do, may, will, have*.

bibliography

(a) a list of works referred to or found useful in the preparation of an essay or report; (b) a reference book listing works available in a particular subject.

case

the inflected form of pronouns (see **inflection**). **Subjective case**: *I, we, he, she, it, they*. **Objective case**: *me, us, him, her, it, them*. **Possessive case**: *my , our, his, her, its, their*.

circumlocution

a roundabout or circuitous expression: e.g., *in a family way* for *pregnant*; *at this point in time* for *now*.

clause

a group of words containing a subject and predicate. An **independent clause** can stand by itself as a complete sentence: e.g., *I bought a hamburger*. A **subordinate** or **dependent clause** cannot stand by itself but must be connected to another clause: e.g., **Since I was hungry,** *I bought a hamburger*.

cliché

a trite or well-worn expression that has lost its impact through overuse: e.g., *slept like a log, sunny disposition, tried and true*.

collective noun

a noun that is singular in form but refers to a group: e.g., *family, team, jury*. It may take either a singular or a plural verb, depending on whether it refers to individual members or to the group as a whole.

comma splice

see **run-on sentence**.

complement

a completing word or phrase that usually follows a linking verb to form a **subjective** complement: e.g., (1) *He is* **my father**. (2) *That cigar smells* **terrible**. If the complement is an adjective it is sometimes called a **predicate adjective**. An **objective complement** completes the direct object rather than the subject: e.g., *We found him* **honest and trustworthy**.

complex sentence

a sentence containing a dependent clause as well as an independent one: e.g., *I bought the ring, although it was expensive*.

compound sentence

a sentence containing two or more independent clauses: e.g., *I saw the car wreck and I reported it*. A sentence is called **compound-complex** if it contains a dependent clause as well as two independent ones: e.g., *When the fog lifted, I saw the car wreck and I reported it*.

conclusion

the part of an essay in which the findings are pulled together or implications revealed so that the reader has a sense of closure or completion. In a business report the conclusion is sometimes placed at the front.

concrete language

specific language, giving particular details (often details of sense): e.g., *red, corduroy dress, three long-stemmed roses* (cf. **abstract language**).

conjunction

an uninflected word used to link words, phrases, or clauses. A **coordinating conjunction** (e.g., *and, or, but, for, yet*) links two equal parts of a sentence. A **subordinating conjunction**, placed at the beginning of a subordinate clause, shows the logical dependence of that clause on another: e.g., (1) **Although** *I am poor, I am happy.* (2) **While** *others slept, he studied.* **Correlative conjunctions** are pairs of coordinating conjunctions (see **correlatives**).

conjunctive adverb

a type of adverb that shows the logical relation between the phrase or clause that it modifies and a preceding one: e.g., (1) *I sent the letter; it never arrived,* **however**. (2) *The battery died;* **therefore** *the car wouldn't start.*

connotation

associative meaning; the range of suggestion called up by a certain word. Apparent synonyms, such as *poor* and *underprivileged*, may have different connotations (cf. **denotation**).

context

the text surrounding a particular passage that helps to establish its meaning.

contraction

a word formed by combining and shortening two words: e.g., *isn't, can't, we're.*

coordinate construction

see **correlatives.**

copula verb

see **linking verb**.

correlatives (coordinates)

pairs of coordinating conjunctions: e.g., *either/or, neither/nor, not only/but.*

dangling modifier

a modifying word or phrase (often a participial phrase) that is not grammatically connected to any part of the sentence: e.g., **Walking to school**, *the street was slippery.*

demonstrative pronoun

a pronoun that points out something: e.g., (1) **This** *is his reason.* (2) **That** *looks like my lost earring.* When used to modify a noun or pronoun, a demonstrative pronoun becomes a kind of **pronominal adjective**: e.g., *this hat, those people.*

denotation

the literal or dictionary meaning of a word (cf. **connotation**).

diction

the choice of words with regard to their tone, degree of formality, or register. Formal diction is the language of orations and serious essays. The informal diction of everyday speech or conversational writing can, at its extreme, become slang.

discourse

talk, either oral or written. **Direct discourse** gives the actual words spoken or written: e.g., *Donne said,* **"No man is an island."** In writing, direct discourse is put in quotation marks.

Indirect discourse gives the meaning of the speech rather than the actual words. In writing, indirect discourse is not put in quotation marks: e.g., *He said that no one exists in an island of isolation.*

ellipsis marks
three spaced periods indicating an omission from a quoted passage.

endnote
a footnote or citation placed at the end of an essay or report.

essay
a literary composition on any subject. Some essays are descriptive or narrative, but in an academic setting most are expository (explanatory) or argumentative.

expletive
a grammatically meaningless exclamation or phrase. The most common expletives are the sentence beginnings *It is* and *There is (are).*

exploratory writing
the informal writing done to help generate ideas before formal planning begins.

footnote
a citation placed at the bottom of a page or the end of the composition (cf. **endnote**).

fused sentence
see **run-on sentence**.

general language
language lacking specific details; abstract language.

gerund
a verbal (part-verb) that functions as a noun and is marked by an *-ing* ending: e.g., **Swimming** *can help you become fit.*

grammar
a study of the forms and relations of words, and of the rules governing their use in speech and writing.

hypothesis
a supposition or trial proposition made as a starting point for further investigation.

hypothetical instance
a supposed occurrence; often shown by a clause beginning with *if.*

indefinite article
see **article**.

independent clause
see **clause**.

indirect discourse
see **discourse**.

infinitive
a type of verbal not connected to any subject: e.g., *to ask*. The **base infinitive** omits the *to*: e.g., *ask*.

inflection
the change in the form of a word to indicate number, person, case, tense, or degree.

integrate
combine or blend together.

intensifier (qualifier)
a word that modifies and adds emphasis to another word or phrase: e.g.,**very** *tired*, **quite** *happy*, *I* **myself**.

interjection

a remark or exlamation interposed or thrown into a speech, usually accompanied by an exclamation mark: e.g., *Oh dear! Alas!*

interrogative sentence

a sentence that asks a question: e.g., *What is the time?*

intransitive verb

a verb that does not take a direct object: e.g., *fall, sleep, talk.*

italics

slanting type used for emphasis, replaced in typescript by underlining.

jargon

technical terms used unnecessarily or in inappropriate places: e.g., *peer-group interaction* for *friendship.*

linking verb (copula verb)

the verb *to be* used to join subject to complement: e.g., *The apples* **were** *ripe.*

literal meaning

the primary, or denotative, meaning of a word.

logical indicator

a word or phrase—usually a conjunction or conjunctive adverb— that shows the logical relation between sentences or clauses: e.g., *since, furthermore, therefore.*

misplaced modifier

a word or group of words that causes confusion or misreading because it is not placed next to the element it should modify: e.g., *I* **only** *ate the pie.* [Revised: *I ate* **only** *the pie.*]

modifier

a word or group of words that describes or limits another element in the sentence.

mood

(a) as a grammatical term, the form that shows a verb's function (indicative, imperative, interrogative, or subjunctive);

(b) when applied to literature generally, the state of mind or feeling shown.

non-restrictive modifier

see **restrictive modifier**.

noun

an inflected part of speech marking a person, place, thing, idea, action, or feeling, and usually serving as subject, object, or complement. A **common noun** is a general term: e.g., *dog, paper, automobile.* A **proper noun** is a specific name: e.g., *Mary, Sudbury, Skidoo.*

object

(a) a noun or pronoun that, when it completes the action of a verb, is called a **direct object**: e.g., *He passed the* **puck**. An **indirect object** is the person or thing receiving the direct object: e.g., *He passed the* **puck** (direct object) *to* **Richard** (indirect object).

(b) The noun or pronoun in a group of words beginning with a preposition; pronouns take the objective case: e.g., *at the* house, *about* **her**, *for* **me**.

objective complement

see **complement**.

objectivity

a disinterested stance; a position taken without personal bias or prejudice (cf. **subjectivity**).

outline
with regard to an essay or report, a brief sketch of the main parts; a written plan.

paragraph
a unit of sentences arranged logically to explain or describe an idea, event, or object; usually marked by indentation of the first line.

parallel wording
wording in which a series of items has a similar grammatical form: e.g., *At her marriage my grandmother promised* **to love, to honour, and to obey** *her husband.*

paraphrase
restate in different words.

parentheses
curved lines, enclosing and setting off a passage; not to be confused with square brackets.

parenthetical element
an interrupting word or phrase: e.g., *My musical career,* **if it can be called that,** *consisted of playing the triangle in kindergarten.*

participle
a verbal (part-verb) that functions as an adjective. Participles can be either **present**, usually marked by an *-ing* ending (e.g., *taking*), or **past** (*having taken*); they can also be passive (*having been taken*).

parts of speech
the major classes of words. Some grammarians include only function words (nouns, verbs, adjectives, and adverbs); others also include pronouns, prepositions, conjunctions, and interjections.

passive voice
see **voice**.

past participle
see **participle**.

periodic sentence
a sentence in which the normal order is inverted or an essential element suspended until the very end: e.g., *Out of the house, past the grocery store, through the school yard and down the railroad tracks* **raced the frightened boy**.

person
in grammar, the three classes of personal pronouns referring to the person speaking (first person), person spoken to (second person), and person spoken about (third person). With verbs, only the third person singular has a distinctive form.

personal pronoun
see **pronoun**.

phrase
a unit of words lacking a subject-predicate combination. The most common kind is the **prepositional phrase**—a unit comprising preposition plus object. Some modern grammarians also refer to the **single-word phrase**.

plural
indicating two or more in number. Nouns, pronouns, and verbs all have plural forms.

possessive case
see **case**.

prefix
a syllable placed in front of the root form of a word to make a new word: e.g., *pro-, in-, sub-* (cf. **suffix**).

preposition

a short word heading a unit of words containing an object, thus forming a **prepositional phrase:** e.g., **under** *the tree*, **before** *my time.*

pronoun

a word that stands in for a noun.

punctuation

a conventional system of signs used to indicate stops or divisions in a sentence and to make meaning clearer: e.g., comma, period, semicolon, etc.

reference works

material consulted when preparing an essay or report.

referent (antecedent)

the noun for which a pronoun stands.

relative clause

a clause headed by a relative pronoun: e.g., *the man* **who came to dinner** *is my uncle.*

relative pronoun

who, which, what, that, or their compounds beginning an adjective or noun clause: e.g., *the house* **that** *Jack built*; **whatever** *you say.*

restrictive element

a phrase or clause that identifies or is essential to the meaning of a term: e.g., *The book* **that I need** *is lost.* It should not be set off by commas. A non-restrictive element is not needed to identify the term and is usually set off by commas: e.g., *This book,* **which I got from my aunt,** *is one of my favourites.*

register

the degree of formality in word choice and sentence structure.

run-on sentence

a sentence that goes on beyond the point where it should have stopped. The term covers both the **comma splice** (two sentences joined by a comma) and the **fused sentence** (two sentences joined without any punctuation between them).

sentence

a grammatical unit that includes both a subject and a predicate. The end of a sentence is marked by a period.

sentence fragment

a group of words lacking either a subject or a verb; an incomplete sentence.

simple sentence

a sentence made up of only one clause: e.g., *Joan climbed the tree.*

slang

colloquial speech, not considered part of standard English; often used in a special sense by a particular group: e.g., *gross* for *disgusting*; *gig* as a musician's term.

split infinitive

a construction in which a word is placed between *to* and the base verb: e.g., *to completely finish.*

squinting modifier

a kind of misplaced modifier; one that could be connected to elements on either side, making meaning ambiguous: e.g., *When he wrote the letter* **finally** *his boss thanked him.*

standard English

the English currently spoken or written by literate people over a wide geographical area.

subject

in grammar, the noun or noun equivalent about which something is predicated; that part of a clause with which the verb agrees: e.g., **They** *swim every day when the* **pool** *is open.*

subjectivity

a personal stance, not impartial (cf. **objectivity**).

subjunctive

see **mood**.

subordinate clause

see **clause**.

subordinating conjunction

see **conjunction**.

subordination

making one clause in a sentence dependent on another.

suffix

an addition placed at the end of a word to form a derivative: e.g., *prepare—prepara***tion**; *sing—sing***ing** (cf. **prefix**).

synonym

a word with the same dictionary meaning as another word: e.g., *begin* and *commence.*

syntax

sentence construction; the grammatical relations of words.

tense

the time reference of verbs.

thesis statement

a one-sentence assertion that gives the central argument of an essay or thesis.

topic sentence

the sentence in a paragraph that expresses the main or controlling idea.

theme

a recurring or dominant idea.

transition word

a word that shows the logical relation between sentences or parts of a sentence and thus helps to signal the change from one idea to another: e.g., *therefore, also, accordingly.*

transitive verb

one that takes an object: e.g., *hit, bring, cover.*

usage

accepted practice.

verb

that part of a predicate expressing an action, state of being, or condition, telling what a subject is or does. Verbs inflect to show tense (time). The principal parts of a verb are the three basic forms from which all tenses are made: the base infinitive, the past tense, and the past participle.

verbal

a word that is similar in form to a verb but does not function as one: a participle, a gerund, or an infinitive.

voice

the form of a verb that shows whether the subject acted (active voice) or was acted upon (passive voice): e.g., *He* **hit** *the ball* (active). *The ball* **was hit** *by him* (passive). Only transitive verbs (verbs taking objects) can be passive.

Index